A Book of

COMPETENCY MAPPING

AND

CAREER DEVELOPMENT

For
M.P.M. Semester - IV
As Per Revised Syllabus
Effective from June 2014

Arati Oturkar
B.Sc., M.C.M, MBA (HR)

Sunil Khilari
MCA, MBA (IT), MCP, DSQM,
ITIL, CTFL, Ph.D (Pursuing)

NIRALI
PRAKASHAN
ADVANCEMENT OF KNOWLEDGE

N2166

MPM - Sem. IV : Competency Mapping & Career Development   ISBN 978-93-5164-266-4

Second Edition   :   January 2016

©   :   Authors

Published By :
NIRALI PRAKASHAN
Abhyudaya Pragati, 1312, Shivaji Nagar
Off J.M. Road, Pune – 411005
Tel - (020) 25512336/37/39, Fax - (020) 25511379
Email : niralipune@pragationline.com

Printed By :
Repro Knowledgecast Limited,
Thane

✦ DISTRIBUTION CENTRES

PUNE

Nirali Prakashan   :   119, Budhwar Peth, Jogeshwari Mandir Lane, Pune 411002, Maharashtra
Tel : (020) 2445 2044, 66022708, Fax : (020) 2445 1538
Email : bookorder@pragationline.com, niralilocal@pragationline.com

Nirali Prakashan   :   S. No. 28/27, Dhyari, Near Pari Company, Pune 411041
Tel : (020) 24690204 Fax : (020) 24690316
Email : dhyari@pragationline.com, bookorder@pragationline.com

MUMBAI

Nirali Prakashan   :   385, S.V.P. Road, Rasdhara Co-op. Hsg. Society Ltd.,
Girgaum, Mumbai 400004, Maharashtra
Tel : (022) 2385 6339 / 2386 9976, Fax : (022) 2386 9976
Email : niralimumbai@pragationline.com

✦ DISTRIBUTION BRANCHES

JALGAON

Nirali Prakashan   :   34, V. V. Golani Market, Navi Peth, Jalgaon 425001,
Maharashtra, Tel : (0257) 222 0395, Mob : 94234 91860

KOLHAPUR

Nirali Prakashan   :   New Mahadvar Road, Kedar Plaza, 1st Floor Opp. IDBI Bank
Kolhapur 416 012, Maharashtra. Mob : 9850046155

NAGPUR

Pratibha Book Distributors   :   Above Maratha Mandir, Shop No. 3, First Floor,
Rani Jhanshi Square, Sitabuldi, Nagpur 440012, Maharashtra
Tel : (0712) 254 7129

DELHI

Nirali Prakashan   :   4593/21, Basement, Aggarwal Lane 15, Ansari Road, Daryaganj
Near Times of India Building, New Delhi 110002
Mob : 08505972553

BENGALURU

Pragati Book House   :   House No. 1, Sanjeevappa Lane, Avenue Road Cross,
Opp. Rice Church, Bengaluru – 560002.
Tel : (080) 64513344, 64513355,Mob : 9880582331, 9845021552
Email:bharatsavla@yahoo.com

CHENNAI

Pragati Books   :   9/1, Montieth Road, Behind Taas Mahal, Egmore,
Chennai 600008 Tamil Nadu, Tel : (044) 6518 3535,
Mob : 94440 01782 / 98450 21552 / 98805 82331,
Email : bharatsavla@yahoo.com

niralipune@pragationline.com | www.pragationline.com

Also find us on www.facebook.com/niralibooks

Dedication

"Dedicated to My Family,
And
My Parents"
And Special Dedication To My
Daughters,
Shreya and Tanisha

Preface ...

This book was written for the thousands of students pursuing MPM degree course. It is full of insights about the fundamentals of Competency Mapping and Career Development.

It covers competency mapping which is about identifying behaviours and personal skills which distinguish excellent and outstanding performance. It also involves identifying key competencies required by a team at a lower level and by the organisation as a whole to achieve desired results. Competency mapping generally involves examining two areas i.e. emotional intelligence and other individual strengths like decision making, team work, performing under pressure etc.

A basic understanding of Competency mapping concepts is not only important for people who want to pursue a career in today's business, business administration or business survival and growth, but it is equally important for people in the organisation who want to achieve desired results as a competency is an underlying characteristic of an individual which enables him/her to deliver superior performance in a given situation. Competencies consist of clusters of knowledge, attitude and skill set. It is the assessment of employee skill set as an individual and as part of a team. Competency mapping is a process of identifying key competencies for a particular position in an organisation, and then using it for job-evaluation, recruitment, training and development, performance management, succession planning.

Some of the important topics covered by this book include the competency models, Delphi Technique, Components of Competency, issues in career development methods etc.

There are a plethora of books that cover the competency mapping understanding & practices but most of these books are generalised reference books and fail to cover all the topics as per the syllabus. Given the rising cost of books and college fees, our student fraternity is generally not in a position to buy several books for one subject. Providing a one stop solution to our students has been the driving force for writing this book.

To make the topics easy to understand the authors have tried to find easiest examples. Important exam oriented questions have been given at the end of each chapter.

Good luck in your endeavours!

Arati Oturkar
Sunil Khilari

Acknowledgement...

We take this opportunity with much pleasure to express our gratitude towards all the people who have helped us through the course of our journey towards producing this book. We sincerely thank Amey Pasalkar, Secretary Sankalp Business School and Mrinmayee Pasalkar,Treasurer Sankalp Business School, who has not only been a guiding spirit for us but has given us an opportunity for coming forward and producing this book.

We are also sincerely thankful to Director, Sankalp Business School and Mr. Amol Kalaskar, Mrs. Vaishnavi Karhadkar who not only guided us on the subject but from whom we have learnt a lot which will surely be useful in different stages of our life and career.

We would also like to express our gratitude to our publishers M/s Nirali Prakashan, who have shown confidence in us and gave us this wonderful opportunity.

Last but not the least, a big thank you to our friends who helped us.

Arati Oturkar
Sunil Khilari

Syllabus ...

1. **History and Origin of Competency:** [7 + 2]

    KSA V/s Competency Reasons for Popularity of Competency, Competency and EVA, Views against Competency, Definitions, Confusion about Competency.

2. **Components of Competency:** [7 + 2]

    Skill, Knowledge and Motive, Trait and Self-Concept, Iceberg Model of Competency, Operant and Respondent Traits of Competency, Competency Models, Leadership and Managerial Competency Models, Causes for Resistance and Recommended Actions to Address, Delphi Technique Competencies and Generic Indicators, 360 Degree Feedback, HR Generic Competency Model, Supervisory Generic Competency Model.

3. **Competency Categories:** [7 + 2]

    Threshold Competencies, Differentiating Competencies, Generic or Key Competencies, Functional or Technical Competencies, Leadership or Managerial Competencies, Steps in Developing Competency Model, Determining the Objective and Scope, Clarifying Implementation Goals and Standards, Create an Action Plan, Define-Performance. Effectiveness Criteria, Identify a Criterion Sample, Data Gathering and Interim Competency Model, Finalize and Validate Competency Model.

4. **Career Development:** [7 + 2]

    Theoretical Foundations, Objectives, Definition of Career Development, Process of Career Planning

    Reasonability for Career Planning and Career Development Methods of Career Development (Management), Competency Approach to Development, Career Paths, Career Transition, Competency Approach to Development.

5. **Innovative Employer Career Initiatives:** [7 + 2]

    Different methods used by Employer to Enhance Employee Career, Special Issues in Career Development, Mentoring for Employee Development.

Contents ...

1. History and Origin of Competency   1.1 – 1.24

2. Components of Competency   2.1 – 2.32

3. Competency Categories   3.1 – 3.20

4. Career Development   4.1 – 4.24

5. Innovative Employer Career Initiatives   5.1 – 5.20

Case Studies   C.1 – C.8

April 2015   P.1 – P.1

Chapter **1**

History and Origin of Competency

Contents ...

1.1 Introduction

1.2 Competency

    1.2.1 Meaning and Definitions of Competency

    1.2.2 Characteristics of Competencies

    1.2.3 Types of Competencies

    1.2.4 Levels of Competencies

    1.2.5 Skills and Competencies

    1.2.6 History and Origin of Competency

    1.2.7 KSA v/s Competency

    1.2.8 Reasons for Popularity of Competency

    1.2.9 Competency and EVA

    1.2.10 Views against Competency

    1.2.11 Examples of Competencies

    1.2.12 Differences between "Skill" and "Competency"

    1.2.13 Competencies are required regardless of industry

    1.2.14 Confusion about Competency

1.3 Competency Mapping

    1.3.1 Need for Competency Mapping

    1.3.2 Steps in Competency Mapping

    1.3.3 Methods of Competency Mapping

    1.3.4 Approaches in Competency Mapping in Human Resource Management

- Points to Remember
- Questions for Discussion
- Project Questions

Learning Objectives ...

➢ To appreciate the importance of competency mapping

➢ To study the difference between KSA and competency

➢ To understand why competency has gained such an enormous importance in recent years

1.1 Introduction

Today organisations are all conversing in terms of competence. Gone are the days when people used to talk in terms of skill sets, which would make their organisations more competitive. There has been a shift in the focus of the organisations. Now they believe in excelling and not competing. It is better to build a core competency that will see them through crisis by developing people, for human resource is the most valuable resource any organisation has. Organisations of the future will have to rely more on their competent employees than any other resource. This is the major factor that determines the success of an organisation.

Competencies are the inner instruments for motivating employees, directing systems and processes and guiding the business towards common goals that allow the organisations to increase its value. Competencies offer a common language and method that can incorporate all the major HR functions and services like recruitment, training, performance management, remuneration, performance appraisal, career and succession planning and integrated human resource management system. Over the last few years, human resource and organisational development professionals have generated a lot of interest in the notion of competencies as a key element and measure of human performance. Adequate resources are spent and consultants are encouraged to do competency mapping. Competency mapping is gaining much more importance and organisations are aware of having better human resources or putting the right people on the right job.

Competency mapping is important and is a fundamental exercise. Every well-managed firm should have well identified roles and record of competencies required to perform each role effectively. Such lists should be used for recruitment, performance management, promotions, placements and training needs identification. In performing or carrying out work, it is essential the required job skills are first articulated. This information not only helps to identify individuals who have the matching skills for doing the work but also the skills that will improve the successful performance of the work. Many times, to perform well, it is not adequate just to have these skills. It is also critical to harmonise the skills with the necessary knowledge and attitudes. For example, the necessary knowledge will enable an individual to apply the right skills for any work situation that will arise while having the right approach will motivate him to give his best efforts. These skills, knowledge and attitudes, required for the work, are usually and collectively referred to as competencies.

Competencies can be motives, traits, self-concept, attitudes or values, content knowledge, or cognitive or behavioural skills. Any individual characteristic that can be measured reliably and shown to differentiate significantly among superior and average performers is competency.

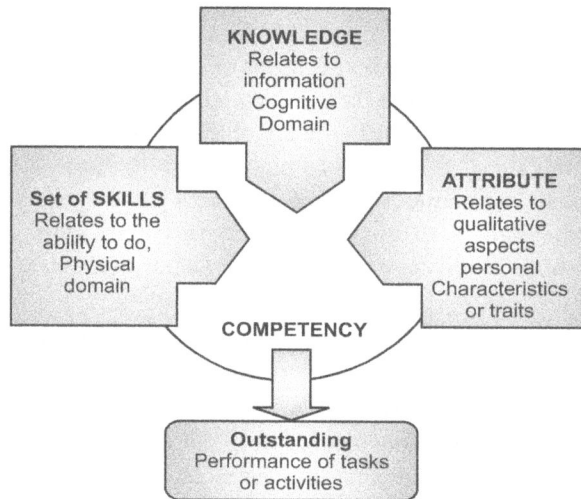

Fig. 1.1: Components of Competency

1.2 Competency

1.2.1 Meaning and Definitions of Competency

Competency is defined as *the process of identifying key attributes and skills for each position and process within the company.*

Another definition would be *Competency is an underlying characteristic required to perform a given task, activity, or role.*

Competence specifies sufficiency of knowledge and skills that enables someone to act in a wide variety of situations. Since each level of responsibility has its own requirements, competence can occur in any period of a person's life or at any stage of his or her career.

Competency is the capability to apply or use a set of related knowledge, skills, and abilities required to successfully perform "critical work functions" or tasks in a defined work setting. Competencies often serve as the basis for skill standards that specify the level of knowledge, skills, and abilities required for success in the workplace as well as potential measurement criteria for assessing competency attainment.

*According to **Hayes** (1979)* – Competencies are generic knowledge motive, trait, social role or a skill of a person linked to superior performance on the job.

*According to **Albanese** (1989)* – Competencies are personal characteristics that contribute to effective managerial performance.

*According to **UNIDO** (2002)* – Competency is a set of skills, related knowledge and attributes that allow an individual to successfully perform a task or an activity within a specific function or job.

1.2.2 Characteristics of Competencies

Competencies have five characteristics namely

1. **Motives:** Things a person consistently thinks about or wants, that cause action, motive, drive, direct and select behavior towards certain actions. For example, achievement motivation makes people consistently set challenging goals for themselves, take responsibility for accomplishing them, and use the feedback to do better.

2. **Traits:** Physical characteristics and consistent responses to situations are known as traits. Good eyesight is a required physical trait in a pilot. Emotional self-control and initiative are more complex, consistent responses to situations.

3. **Self-concept:** Self-concept is person's attitude value or self-image. A person's values are reactive or respondent motives that predict what a person would do in the short run. For example, a person who values being a leader would be more likely to exhibit leadership behaviour.

4. **Knowledge:** Knowledge is the information a person has in a specific work area, for example, an accountant's knowledge of various accounting procedures.

5. **Skill:** Skill is the ability to perform certain mental or physical tasks using analytical thinking. In other words, it is the ability to establish cause and affect relationship.

1.2.3 Types of Competencies

1. **Managerial Competencies** are considered essential for staff with managerial or supervisory responsibility in any service or program area, including directors and senior posts.

   Some managerial competencies could be more relevant for specific occupations. However, they are applied horizontally across the organisation, i.e. analysis and decision-making, team leadership, change management, etc.

2. **Generic Competencies** are considered essential for all staff, regardless of their function or level, i.e. communication, program execution, processing tools, linguistic, etc.

3. **Technical/Functional Competencies** are specific competencies considered essential to perform any job in the organisation within a defined technical or functional area of work, i.e. environmental management, industrial process sectors, investment management, finance and administration, human resource management, etc.

1.2.4 Levels of Competencies

1. **Practical Competency:** An employee has demonstrated ability to perform a set of tasks.

2. **Foundational Competence:** An employee has demonstrated understanding of the reason for the task to be done.

3. **Reflexive Competence:** An employee's ability to integrate actions with the understanding of the action, so that he/she learns from those actions and adapts to the changes as and when required.

4. **Applied Competence:** An employee's demonstrated ability to perform a set of tasks with understanding and reflexivity.

1.2.5 Skills and Competencies

The terms skills and competencies are used interchangeably. In fact, with many HR practitioners, competencies seem to relate only to "behavioural" competencies as defined in a competency dictionary.

1. **Skill:** Skill is a proficiency, capability, or agility that is acquired or developed through training or experience; the ability coming from one's knowledge, practice, aptitude, etc., to do somewhat well. It is an ability and capacity acquired through deliberate, organised, and sustained effort to smoothly and adaptively carry out complex activities or job functions involving ideas (cognitive skills), things (technical skills), and/or people (interpersonal skills). A skill is the learned capacity to carry out pre-determined consequences, and a learned capability to bring about the required results with maximum certainty and efficiency.

2. **Competency:** Refers to a cluster of related abilities, commitments, knowledge, and skills that enable a person (or an organisation) to act effectively in a job or situation. Competencies refer to skills or knowledge that leads to superior performance. They are measurable skills, abilities and personality traits that categorise successful employees in definite roles within an organisation. A competency is more than just knowledge and skills. **It involves the ability to meet complex demands, by drawing on and activating psychosocial resources (including skills and attitudes) in a particular circumstance**. It is a measurable pattern of knowledge, skills, abilities, behaviours and other characteristics an individual needs to perform work roles or occupational functions successfully. Competencies specify the "how", as opposed to "what" of performing job tasks or what the person needs to do to carry out the job successfully.

1.2.6 History and Origin of Competency

In the last century, business has come full circle in its attitude towards workplace competencies. In the beginning of the twentieth century, work brought complex skills to the job. Typical business processes required specific competencies for the task at hand. These competencies could be acquired only through years of on-the-job learning and practice.

Then came the era of scientific management where Frederick Taylor and Henry Ford's use of assembly lines shifted competencies from workers to time-and-motion study. Complexity was minimised and efficiency was maximised. In a depression economy, employees had little value. Process expertise left little scope for training. If the worker could not handle the monotony, boredom, or physical strain, a large number of applicants were available to fill openings,

Later, in the mid-century, World War II enforced management centric views where officers gave orders to subordinates who obeyed the commands without questions. Thus, somebody had to run things and only those in command were assumed to have the information, perspective and abilities to make decisions.

After the war, they still lived under a command and control hierarchy. Specialists had the tasks broken into smaller tasks. In the post-war decade, the demand was unparalleled and competition was little. The turnaround came in the early 1960s when **McClelland** wrote a landmark article in the American Psychologist asserting that IQ and personality tests that were then in common use were predictors of competency. He felt that companies should hire people based upon competencies rather than test scores.

Later McClelland, founder of McBer, a consulting company, was asked by the US Information Agency (USIA) to develop new methods that could predict human performance. The objective was to eliminate the potential biases of traditional intelligence and aptitude testing. This was the beginning of the field of competence measurement.

The next step was for competency concepts to find their way into mainstream business practices.

McClelland (1973) began by asking the USIA's personnel director and some top managers for the names of their most outstanding employees. He also asked for the names of people whose jobs were secure but who were in no way outstanding.

To differentiate between the two groups, McClelland and his colleague asked fifty people to describe three incidents where they felt they had outstanding performance and where they felt they had really messed up. To establish a clear picture, minute details were asked for what was said, what was done, when and where it all happened, who else was there and so on. These detailed descriptions enabled them to find out a pattern of what competencies the outstanding performers had demonstrated which others had not.

Many of the skills that the panel of experts had identified as crucial to job performance turned out to be irrelevant to the everyday duties of the people interviewed by McClelland.

In order to validate the conclusions about which competencies were necessary McClelland tested them on another group of officers who had been identified as outstanding and a group who fell into the mediocre category. Using psychological tests for the key competencies, he found that the officers identified as outstanding consistently performed very well on such tests, whereas those rated mediocre performed poorly. Thus, it was clear that the key competencies identified were indeed relevant to job performance.

The turning point for competency movement is the article published in America in 1973 by McClelland. In this article, he presented data that traditional achievement, intelligence scores may not be able to predict job success, and what is required is to profile the exact competencies required to perform a given job effectively and measure them using a variety of tests. Equally noteworthy is the pioneering work by Douglas Brey and his associates at AT&T in the US, which gave evidence that competencies could be assessed through assessment centres and on-the-job success could be predicted to some extent. Both these researches laid the foundation for popularisation of the competency movement.

Later McBer, a consulting firm founded by David McClelland and his associate David Berlew, specialised in mapping the competencies of entrepreneurs and managers across the world. They even developed a new and yet simple methodology called the Behaviour Event Interviewing (BEI) to map the competencies. The AT&T Studies of Formative Years in Business indicated the predictability of future success. McClelland's studies in the early seventies indicated the limitations of intelligence and academic performance data.

With increased recognition of the limitations of performance appraisal in predicting future performances, potential appraisal was focused and assessment centers became popular in the seventies. Setting up an assessment centre was an integral part of the HRD plan given to IAVT by the 11MA professors as early as in 1975. L&T did competency mapping and could not start assessment centres until much later as it was not perceived as a priority area.

1.2.7 KSA v/s Competency

KSA (Knowledge, Skills and Abilities) is a list of special qualifications and personal attributes that a candidate needs to have for a particular job. These are the unique requirements that the hiring agency wants to find in the person selected to fill a particular job. A primary purpose of KSAs is to measure those qualities that will set one candidate apart from the others. KSAs are defined as the factors that identify the better candidates from a group of people qualified for a position. How well an applicant can show that he or she matches the position's defined KSAs determine whether that person will be seriously considered for the job.

1. **Knowledge** statements refer to an organised body of information usually of a factual or procedural nature, which, if applied, makes adequate performance on the job possible; a body of information applied directly to the performance of a function.

2. **Skill** statements refer to the proficient manual, verbal or mental manipulation of data or things. Skills can be readily measured by a performance test where quantity and quality of performance are tested, usually within an established time limit. Examples of proficient manipulation of things are skill in typing or skill in operating a vehicle. Examples of proficient manipulation of data are skill in computation using decimals; skill in editing of transposed numbers, etc.

3. **Ability** statements refer to the power to perform an observable activity now. This means that abilities have been evidenced through activities or behaviours that are similar to those required on the job, e.g., ability to plan and organise work. Abilities are different from aptitudes. Aptitudes are only the potential for performing the activity.

KSA	Competencies
It struggles with performance and behaviour standards.	Performance standards identified.
There is a lack of standardisation.	Packs a lot of detail in each punch.
Judges are familiar with them and know what to look for.	Counters KSA well and adds more value with detailed behavioural descriptors.
There is lack in detailing.	Leaves no question as to what is described.
Simple to write, read, and understand.	Difficult to read quickly.

1.2.8 Reasons for Popularity of Competency

'Competency' and 'competencies' may be defined as the behaviours (and, where appropriate, technical attributes) that individuals must have, or must acquire, to perform effectively at work that is, the terms focus on the individual attributes or inputs of the individual.

'Competence' and 'competences' are broader concepts that include demonstrable performance outputs as well as behaviour inputs, and may relate to a system or set of minimum standards required for effective performance at work.

A 'competency framework' is a structure that sets out and defines each individual competency (such as problem solving or people management) required by individuals working in an organisation or part of an organisation.

The concept of competency as a feature in recruitment, selection, hiring and employee performance evaluation has become very famous not only among HR practitioners but to the management as well. Yet, in more than three decades while it became a buzzword, still many are unfamiliar with the details of the concept such as its apt application and utility.

Competency is still equated or defined as skills, ability to perform, capacity, and knowledge. As such, the term has been used loosely. While it does not really matter much when used casually to mean physical and mental abilities, it does matter when used in job analysis to describe job requirements and performance standards. Competency takes more than skills and knowledge. It requires the right and appropriate attitude that eventually translates to behaviour.

Competency is the sum total of skills, knowledge and attitudes, manifested in the employee's behaviour. It is the "means" to achieve the "ends". A computer service customer representative may be very skillful and knowledgeable in repairing computers, but if he does not arrive at an appointed time to the client, is similarly incompetent.

Use of competencies has been increasing in popularity due to following reasons.

- These days jobs are increasingly being described in terms of the expertise required to do them rather than simply in terms of the tasks or psychological processes entailed.

- Organisations are unhappy with the lack of consistency in recruitment and development.

- The traditional fixed boundaries stuck between different jobs are dissolving.

- The traditional hierarchical structures within organisations are vanishing.

- There has been a definite decrease in the stability and certainty of jobs.

- Competencies are often cheaper and more user friendly to implement than psychometric assessment.

The correct identification of the competencies involved in a particular job is the most critical part of the selection or development system, and it is essential they are clearly specified with the help of using a structured and defensible job analysis technique. An indistinct or imprecise idea of the competencies required will promise failure.

The benefits of an organisation-specific competency model include

- The specification of a visible set of agreed standards.
- It can proceed as a model for improving all aspects of recruitment and development.
- It specifies what selectors ought to be assessing in an aspirant.
- It provides the foundation for the design of all assessment activity.
- It removes the subjectivity and personal bias from assessment and performance evaluation.
- It not only facilitates the evaluation of validity, reliability, and fairness but also the cost benefits.
- It gives a sense of ownership of the competency list.
- It portrays competencies in language that is relevant to the organisations.
- It improves the chances of hiring the right person.
- It also provides a baseline for evaluating performance.
- Gives an insight into the training needs of a position.

While you drill down the drivers of performance for most organisations, things like great customer service, efficient processes, and empowering technology, you reach a base level for making these drivers happen. This gets you back to the qualities of your human resources – knowledge, expertise, experience, and those things needed for successful execution. The combination of skills, expertise, knowledge and other intangibles will differ from job to job. One of the more powerful tools for capturing the characteristics behind critical functions is the competency model. Not only does the competency model neatly systematise success factors behind a position, but it also describes the behaviour needed for maximum performance. Competency models can represent a key component for building an overall HR system. For example, we can use competency models for applying the same standards throughout the company. This helps diminish bias and unfairness in how we evaluate performance.

Finally, the best forms of competencies (knowledge, skills, etc.) tend to be behaviours. Behaviours are easier to take hold of and understand. Employees tend to recognise acceptable behaviours as opposed to improving their skill sets. Once employees have reached behavioural thresholds, they move to higher skills such as leadership to drive long-term employee performance.

"Competency models are a means of ensuring that your investment in your people supports the achievement of strategic goals. The popularity of competency modeling is steadily increasing. Human resource professionals and line managers everywhere are now using competency models to make wise decisions about selection and placement, as well as training and development and performance management." - The Art and Science of Competency Models by Antoinette D. Lucia and Richard Lepsinger.

1.2.9 Competency and EVA

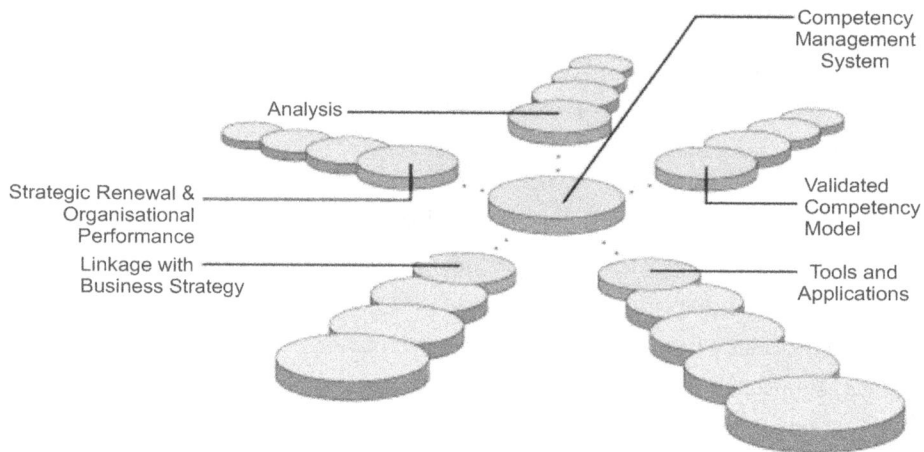

Fig. 1.2: Competency and EVA

How can shareholders consistently expect executives to create value and wealth for their organisations, and compensate executives based on value creation without ensuring that such value creating qualities and competencies are innate to executives? In recent years, maximising shareholder value has become the new and widely accepted corporate paradigm. Studies by Sternetal (1991) and Stewart (1991, 1994) pioneered the development of Economic Value Added (EVA), a financial measurement for real economic value. These studies assert that EVA stands well out in the crowd as the single best measure of value creation for an organisation on a continuous basis. Ward and Price (2008) also support this idea. Subsequent to the establishment of EVA, many studies have reported the different uses and adoptions of EVA. These studies are reflected in the work of Sharma and Kumar (2010). It is of significance that these previous studies acknowledge the link between economic value creation, executive's performance, and further recognise how the executives' performance is linked to their compensation. Noble as it sounds, these studies have limitations with regard to the role of competencies in the executive's development process and value creation.

The most fundamental blemish lies in the fact that there seems to be no strategic link between EVA as a performance measure and the capability of executives to create value in organisations. It is difficult for organisations to bring to light the proposition that cannot measure what was never assessed. As an outcome there needs to be further exploration as to why there is a disjuncture between executive performance and executive competency with regard to the utilisation of the EVA metric. The main concept is that there should be competencies that are inherent towards developing shareholders value.

1. Competency mapping is actually done for management staff.

2. Competency mapping is based on KSAs (Knowledge, Skills and Attitudes).

3. The other factors for which competencies mapping is based on are

   • Work ethics

   • Values

   • Communication ability

4. Competency mapping is done by defining the job descriptions and the skills required for those job descriptions.

5. When the rating of the superior does not match with the actual rating, that employee, whose competencies are mapped, goes for further training.

1.2.10 Views against Competency

There are various views against competency. A problem with competency mapping, especially when conducted by few organisations, is that there may be no scope for an individual to work in a field that would best make use of his or her competencies.

An additional problem is that competency models are sometimes too idealistic and ambitious for the workforce. The following are certain views against competency.

   • **It is impossible to capture realistic competencies:** This means it is possible to capture knowledge and skills as a part of competency but not the behavioural dimension of competency, because it is vibrant and unseen.

   • **Competency approach is hardly an intellectual thing:** Competency is more of a theoretical concept than a practical one.

   • **It is not a reliable indicator:** Many managers and critics are of the opinion that competency modelling and assessment exercises are not reliable indicators of actual performance, e.g. some employees with high intelligent quotient can be in reality poor performers.

- **Competency causes shift in focus:** Employees tend to believe that they merely need to demonstrate their competencies and proficiencies, and they need not actually apply them at work. It creates more of learning than of productivity.

- **Competency is capital intensive:** Competency mapping modelling and assessment involve huge expenses and budgetary requirements. Not all organisations can afford to implement them.

- **Competency breeds homogeneity:** One of the major drawbacks of the competency approach is it kills diversity and heterogeneity and promotes everybody, identical in behaviour, thus overlooking innovation and creativity.

1.2.11 Examples of Competencies

A competency is a feature that a company believes is desirable for its workforce to have. Competencies can be global or specific. Global competencies are broad in nature, and are qualities that all employees within an organisation should have. Specific competencies are qualities that are unique to a position or field within the organisation. Some examples of global competencies are

1. **Communication:** This competency includes listening skills, presenting, and clearly expressing ideas in an oral and written format.

2. **Teamwork:** The skills needed in this competency can include convincing, helping, listening, and getting along with others in a team.

3. **Responsibility:** Depending on the organisation, this competency can refer to social responsibility (community involvement, green operations) or it can refer to accountability.

4. **Commitment to career:** The skills in this competency involve knowledge of an industry or firm such that the employee can clearly articulate the role he/she plays in the organisation.

5. **Leadership:** This competency involves the skills needed to organise, motivate and/or develop others.

6. **Industry awareness:** The knowledge contained in this competency refers to a general knowledge of business practices, and the industry in which they are working.

7. **Career motivation:** This competency involves the level of desire to work in a specific organisation and includes training or experience that can be received.

8. **Decision-making:** The skills needed in this competency include defining the issue, fact-gathering, considering possible solutions and selecting the best option.

9. **Organisational skills:** This competency involves the skills needed to manage time appropriately, set priorities and tasks.

10. **Result-oriented:** This competency refers to the ability to meet objectives in time, balancing both cost and quality and is easily measurable as it is entirely performance based.

11. **Problem solving:** The goal of this competency is to overcome obstacles to meet a stated goal and involves discovering and analysing problems.

As stated above, specific competencies are exclusive to a field or position. Some examples could include knowledge of general accounting practices for an accountant, excellent telephone skills for a call centre employee or negotiating skills for a public prosecutor.

To summarise, competencies are qualities and skills that an employer has identified as crucial for its workforce. Competencies can be global (held across the entire organisation) or specific (exclusive to a field or position). The examples of competencies in the list above cannot not be considered as all-inclusive. Instead, the examples of global competencies given should be a starting point for an employer to determine the competencies vital to its organisational development.

1.2.12 Differences between "Skill" and "Competency"

- **Definition.** In fact, some "skills" may be "competencies" in other organisations. They are not black and white items that HR can fit in all places for all things.
- **Skills are** something you know and learn, and something "tangible." These two answers were generally agreed upon to try getting some structure around this question. One can argue that skills are the *"nuts and bolts"* of what a person does in their roles within an organisation.
- **Competencies are** the effective application of skills.

1.2.13 Competencies are required regardless of industry.

- **Intentional communication:** Before one jumps to the conclusion that "communication is skill", lets take a different look. If employees were more forthright and intentional in their communication efforts, that would be a broader approach. Too much of today's communication is hidden and guarded. Being intentional is a competency that could change the look of most company cultures.
- **Integrity:** This is important in a society that is growing so skeptical day by day. People still want people to be honest. To know that an employee gives out genuine integrity is priceless and needed in today's challenging workplace environments.
- **Character:** Similar to integrity, people want to work with others who are genuine. Being genuine is desired, but is it valued? It is true that a strong character shows drive, initiative, and engagement. However, how character is defined in the workplace is up to the workplace involved.

- **Emotional intelligence:** Emotional intelligence is required in all organisations. The difficulty is it is still an area that is too broad and open to interpretation. Another way to look at it is to make it even more "human." We want employees who show the ability to be empathetic, adaptable, and open to meeting people where "they are." Getting employees that show an "others-focused" competency as against the overwhelming "self-focused" reality we struggle with would be refreshing.

1.2.14 Confusion about Competency

This word competency is a very popular word used by different persons in the industry. When used by different people it is as good as the shape and size of a blind man's perception of an elephant. People also interchangeably use the word competence to capability. This lucid use of such terms creates more confusion.

Most selection systems are now competency or behaviour based. Competencies are rapidly emerging as the future of occupational assessment and much of our selection system design work now revolves around their use. This is based on the principle the best way of predicting job success is to identify the behaviours required in a job and then give an individual tasks to do that are representative of the types of behaviour they might have to do in a particular job (job simulations), or direct samples of the activities that are carried out in that job (work samples). For instance, the term "competency-based learning" is often used synonymously with personalised learning, student-centered learning, and blended learning.

The term 'competence' has been used so widely and so divergently in so many different contexts that it has ceased to have any precise meaning. Different writers interpret it in different ways for different purposes. As a result, there is great confusion about what the term refers to in any given instance. Writers frequently discuss the concept without taking into account the fact that interpretations of it differ greatly. It is suggested that making a clear distinction between 'competence' and 'proficiency' helps to resolve many of these difficulties.

Competency definition would vary from one organisation to another. One obvious reason is that the values of each organisation are not same; also, the business environment has its own peculiarities.

1. **Confusion between Competence and Competency:** Though both the terms are synonymous, there is a subtle difference when they are used. Competency is to identify and assess a personal attribute but competence is to identify the tasks of a job and know the requirements to perform the job.

2. **Confusion between Performance and Competency:** There is always a debate on the difference between performance and competency. The confusion is whether

performance is an indicator of competency or competency is an indicator of performance. In reality, competency is what a person owns in the form of knowledge, skills and attitude, whereas performance is what a person delivers.

3. **Confusion between Core Competence and Competency:** Core competency is an organisational tool used in strategic management. For example, Sony's core competence is in miniaturisation and competency is in the attributes of individuals, their skills and knowledge. So one can understand core competence is an organisational level concept and competency an individual level concept.

People using these terms shape their meaning to fit their own convenience. **RON Zemke's** comments on these terms in 1982 remain valid even today.

"Competency competencies, competency models and competency-based training are Humpty Dumpty words meaning only what the definer want them to mean. The problem comes not from malice, stupidity, or marketing avarice, but instead from, some basic procedural and philosophical differences among those racing to define and develop the concept and to set the model for the way the rest of us will use competencies in our day-to-day effort."

1.3 Competency Mapping

Competency mapping plays an imperative role in selecting, recruiting and retaining the right people. When the competency required for a particular position is mapped, an accurate job profile is created. Competency mapping involves the process by which we determine

- The nature and scope of a specific job position.
- The skills required.
- The depth of knowledge required.
- The behavioural capacities required to apply those skills and knowledge in that role.'

Also,

- Knowledge
- Skills
- Attitude

These three factors are significant for identifying competency in an individual. Different individuals require different competencies. For example, a person working in an IT sector may require different competencies than a person working in a sales sector. Competency varies from industry to industry. According to Harvard Business Review, Daniel Katz grouped competency into three areas, which later expanded into the following four.

- Technical
- Managerial
- Human
- Conceptual

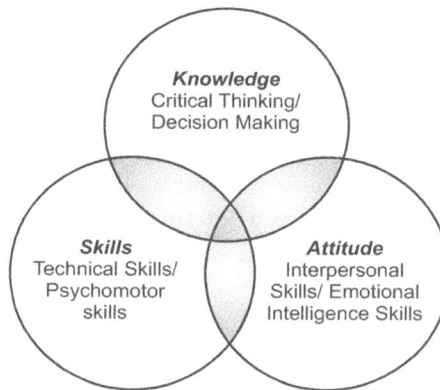

Fig. 1.3: KSA

1.3.1 Need for Competency Mapping

1. Structured and documented procedures provide convenience in recruitment, thereby reducing time and employee cost.

2. Predefined criteria eliminate wrong recruitment, thereby reducing time and employee cost.

3. The organisation has a ready reckoner of skill inventory / management inventory.

4. Tangible and measurable criteria eliminate chances of any sort of bias among employee performances. Hence, the chances of employee conflict or grievances reduce greatly.

5. Training need identification becomes clear and precise.

6. Employees have chances of earning variable pay by enhancing competencies required for the job.

7. Helps in benchmarking standards.

8. Gains a clearer sense of true marketability in today's job market by enabling the individual know his/her competencies compared to those that are required by the job market in key positions of interest.

9. Projects the appearance of a "cutting-edge" and well-prepared candidate who has taken the time to learn about competencies, investigate those in demand and map his/her own competencies prior to the interview.

10. Develops the capability to compare one's actual competencies to an organisation or position's required/preferred competencies, in order to create an individual development plan.

11. Demonstrates self-confidence that comes from knowing one's competitive advantages more convincingly, and from being able to articulate those advantages in a specific language.

1.3.2 Steps in Competency Mapping

The following steps are followed in competency mapping.

1. Decide the positions for which the competencies need to be mapped.

2. Identify the location of the positions in the organisational structure. This needs the clarity of organisational structure, defining the position relationships (reporting authority, subordinates, peers etc.).

3. Identify the objectives of the function or the department or the unit or section where the position is located.

4. Identify the objectives of the role. Why does the position exist? What are the main purposes of the role? etc.

5. Collect the Key Performance Areas (KPAs) of the position holder for the last two to three years from the performance appraisal records. Alternately, collect the job descriptions of the position to make a list of all tasks and activities to be performed by that position holder.

6. Interview the position holder and list the tasks and activities to be performed by the individual. Group them into a set of tasks. The tasks in the list may be as many as 15 to 20 for some positions, few or five to six for other positions. There is no rigid rule about the number of tasks. It depends on how complex the position is. It is useful to start with as many tasks as possible.

7. Interview the position holder to list the actual knowledge, attitude, skills, and other competencies required for performing the task effectively. The position holder has to answer questions like "If you are to recruit someone to perform this task what qualities or competencies would you look for in him/her? What competencies do you think are required to perform this well?

8. Repeat the process with all the members.

9. Consolidate the list of competencies from all the position holders by each task.

10. Edit and finalise. Present it to the supervisors of the position holder for approval and finalisation.

1.3.3 Methods of Competency Mapping

Businesses use competency mapping to match the capabilities and talent of personnel with specific job tasks and organisational needs. The technique involves conducting a job analysis to identify core skills and behaviours required to perform the role, drafting a job description based on the key competencies and aligning resources to best fulfill competency needs. Having a competency map makes it easier for firms to identify qualified candidates, assess performance, focus training efforts and enhance overall productivity. Common competency mapping approaches include assessment centre, critical incidents technique, interviewing, questionnaires and psychometric tests.

1. **Assessment Centre:** The assessment centre methodology involves situational observation to evaluate performance and growth potential of candidates relative to specified job attributes. The approach uses various types of discussion and simulation exercises to reflect real-life demands of the job. Candidates are asked to work through certain scenarios while a trained assessor observes their behaviour. The situations are designed to reveal skills and aptitude that help identify which individuals are good matches for the current and future requirements of the job.

2. **Critical Incidents Technique:** The critical incidents technique uses data gathering and analysis to identify job-specific behaviours that influence the success or failure of an individual or collective business operation performing a certain job. Data about critical events—an exceptional example of accomplishment or failure—is collected through interviews or questionnaires as soon as possible after occurrence. The incidents are then categorised according to associated job behaviours to reveal patterns of performance gaps and strengths.

3. **Interviews:** The candidate interview provides first-hand insight into candidate behaviours and is an effective method for collecting relevant information and impressions about prospective employees. Interviewers should be prepared with targeted questions that not only draw out details about tangible job experiences but also give clues about the candidate's general motivation, disposition and outlook. The interview record can be compared with the competency map created for the job to determine which candidate offers the best match for the organisation's needs.

4. **Questionnaires:** Questionnaires offer another approach for gathering information about job competencies and work performance. Several types used in competency mapping include the common metric questionnaire that highlights work requirements and activities, functional job analysis that describes job duties and characteristics, occupational analysis inventory that specifies work elements for almost all occupations, position analysis questionnaire that ties job characteristics to human characteristics and work profiling system that measures ability and personality attributes. The multipurpose occupational system analysis inventory highlights tasks and competencies for government jobs.

5. **Psychometric Tests:** Psychometric testing provides a consistent approach to measuring and quantifying a sample of behavioral attributes. The two main types of psychometric assessment are aptitude tests and achievement tests. Aptitude tests are used to identify natural inclinations in a specific area, such as art or science, and are designed to help predict how well a person would perform in a given specialty after being provided with training. Achievement tests measure the level of proficiency an individual has achieved in a certain area, such as mathematics, language skills and ability to reason.

1.3.4 Approaches in Competency Mapping in Human Resource Management

1. **Recruitment and Selection:** Competency-based recruitment is a process, based on the ability of candidates to produce anecdotes about their professional experience, which can be taken as evidence that the candidate has a given competency. Candidates demonstrate competencies on the application form, and then in the interview, which in this case, is a competency-based interview.

The process is intended to be fairer than other recruitment processes by clearly laying down the required competencies and then testing them in such a way that the recruiter has little discretion to favour one candidate over another; the process assumes high recruiter discretion undesirable. As a result of its perceived fairness, the process is popular in public services. Competency-based recruitment is highly focused on the candidates' story-telling abilities as an indication of competency, and disfavours other indications of a candidate's skills and potentials, such as references.

A competency-based approach to recruitment and selection of staff can help an organisation to make it an effective and successful investment of time, money and expertise. Such an approach will help ensure the organisation is clear regarding the competencies and skill sets required by the job. Individual skills and abilities are matched to the requirements of the job and evaluation of work demands and staffing are accurate.

2. Performance Management System: Performance management is about achieving results within the stipulated time that is consistent with organisational expectations. Integrating competencies within the performance management process supports the provision of feedback to employees not only on "what" they have accomplished (i.e., performance goals), but also "how" the work was performed, using competencies for providing feedback.

Integrating competency with PMS will assist

(a) Employees in understanding performance expectations and enhancing competencies.

(b) In integrating capabilities with existing or new processes.

(c) In providing positive feedback about an employee's training achievements and on-the-job performance.

(d) In providing job standards for performance appraisal.

(e) In providing a clear direction for learning new job skills.

3. Training: Competency-based training focuses on what the participant is expected to be able to do in the workplace as opposed to just having theoretical knowledge. An important characteristic of competency-based training is that it is focused not only on the actual jobs that are required in the workplace, but also the ability to transfer and apply skills, knowledge and attitudes to new situations and environments.

- The emphasis in competency-based training is on "performing" rather than just "knowing".

- Competence-based programs need to focus on building the knowledge and skills needed in a particular job. Competence-based programs are also used to increase employees' current job performance, prepare them for changing job requirements or introduce new tools or technology in the workplace.

- By having a well-designed competence-based training and development program the organisation will be able to ensure it has the right people, with the right skills, at the right time, to accomplish their business objectives.

The advantages of competency-based training (CBT) are

(i) Participants will achieve competencies required in the performance of their jobs.

(ii) Participants build confidence as they succeed in mastering specific competencies.

(iii) Participants receive a transcript or list of the competencies they have achieved.

4. Development: For organisations to succeed in today's competitive setting, employees at all levels need to develop and demonstrate a set of behaviour showcasing his or her capabilities, characteristics, knowledge, talent as well as personal qualities for effective performance at work.

All businesses are based on some key competencies. If any business neglects employee competency and its development, all growth and productivity of employees, company and profits are affected. The main reason for an organisation to create a competency-based system that focuses on having the right people with right skills at the right time is that it helps in accomplishing business targets.

Competencies are the need of the hour and designing appropriate competency development models is a necessity.

Advantages of competency based development.

(i) Improvement in productivity, performance and profitability.

(ii) Identification of employee's capabilities for an organisation's future needs.

(iii) Analysing capability gaps.

5. Compensation: Competency-based pay fits this new environment. It provides an ongoing incentive to employees to enhance their ability to perform their jobs. Employees are rewarded with salary increases when they add new knowledge or skills or when they demonstrate a higher level of competence on existing capabilities.

Advantages of competency-based compensation.

(i) Provides a base for deciding on the compensation.

(ii) Encourages employees to develop their competencies further.

(iii) Leads to a focus on totality of job rather than just what is achieved.

(iv) This system fits every job.

Points to Remember

- It is a buzzword in current times and a lot is going on in the issue of competency mapping. Many resources are spent and consultants are encouraged to do competency mapping. Competency mapping is gaining much more importance and organisations are aware of having better human resources or putting the right people on right job.

- **Competency mapping** is important and is a fundamental exercise. Every well-managed firm should have well identified roles and a list of competencies required to perform each role effectively. Such a list should be used for recruitment, performance management, promotions, placements and training needs identification.

- Competencies are becoming a frequently-used and written-about vehicle for organisationsal applications such as:

  o Defining the factors for success in jobs (i.e., work) and work roles within the organisations.

  o Assessing the current performance and future development needs of persons holding jobs and roles.

  o Mapping succession possibilities for employees within the organisations.

  o Assigning compensation grades and levels to particular jobs and roles.

  o Selecting applicants for open positions, using competency-based interviewing techniques.

- Competencies include the collection of success factors necessary for achieving important results in a specific job or work role in particular organisations. Success factors are combinations of knowledge, skills, and attributes (more historically called "KSA's") that are described in terms of specific behaviours, and are demonstrated by superior performers in those jobs or work roles. Attributes include personal characteristics, traits, motives, values or ways of thinking that influence an individual's behavior.

Questions for Discussion

1. Define competency. What key role does it play in an organisation's workforce planning?
2. Differentiate between KSA and competency.
3. Why is competency popular in today's world?
4. How are competency and EVA related?
5. What is competency? State the differences between competence and competency.
6. What are the different competencies needed for different administrative and cognitive positions?
7. Which are the global competencies? Explain with examples.

Project Questions

1. A multi-national static metre manufacturer operating in India has retained you. The electricity boards uses Static metres to take the reading and bill the customers. Quality conformance requirements for static metres are very high, with a maximum ± percent tolerance limit. The company requires a competency based performance management system. Develop your line of actions.

2. Do you agree that an exercise in competency mapping is futile and waste of time? Discuss.

■■■

Chapter 2

Components of Competency

Contents ...

2.1   Components of Competency
    2.1.1   Skills
    2.1.2   Knowledge
    2.1.3   Motive
    2.1.4   Traits
    2.1.5   Self-concept
2.2   Iceberg Model of Competency
2.3   Operant and Respondent Traits of Competency
2.4   Competency Models
2.5   Leadership and Managerial Competency Models
    2.5.1   Core Competencies
    2.5.2   Leadership Competencies
    2.5.3   Professional Competencies for Learning/Training Leaders
2.6   Organisational Change
2.7   Delphi Technique
2.8   360-degree Feedback
2.9   HR Generic Competency Model
2.10 Supervisory Generic Competency Model
    •   Points to Remember
    •   Questions for Discussion
    •   Project Questions

Objectives ...

- ➤ To understand the various components of competencies.
- ➤ To study how the iceberg model is helpful to understand hidden skills.
- ➤ To learn various models of competency development.
- ➤ To be able to explain various causes of resistance for change along with recommended actions for the same.

2.1 Components of Competency

Competencies are defined as "skills and abilities, described in behavioural terms that are coachable, observable, measurable and critical to successful individual or organisation performance", while goals are the "what" of performance, and competencies are the "how" of performance.

Competencies are the knowledge, skills and personal attributes required for excellent performance in a job, role or specific business. Competency development is a carefully crafted process of research and data-gathering about the firm's managers and employees as they perform their daily work, with the goal of determining the specific knowledge, skills and personal attributes required for excellent performance in these actual jobs, roles or businesses.

The competencies and the need to develop them translate into a personal development plan and the whole links to what is achieved within the organisation. Severn Trent Water (UK water company) has developed an interesting definition of competency as 'grouping of knowledge, skills and behaviours which may well be required in whole or in part within a variety of managerial situations'. Competency analysis is concerned with the behavioural dimensions of the roles.

Competencies are underlying characteristics of people and indicate "ways of behaving or thinking, generalising across situations, and enduring for a reasonably long period of time."

Competencies are based on

1. Skills

2. Knowledge

3. Motive

4. Traits

5. Self-concept

2.1.1 Skills

Capabilities acquired through practice. Skill is adeptness, capability, or agility acquired or developed through training or experience. A skill is the learned capacity to carry out pre-determined consequences. Skills are learned capabilities to bring about the result you want, with maximum certainty and efficiency. Skill is defined as the ability coming from knowledge, to do something well. It is the manager's responsibility to be acquainted with the difference between 'knowing' and 'doing' and help their field service engineers to develop the skills they need to do their job well. This means that an employee is unlikely to return to the office after training and automatically be skilled at a new task without being given time to practice the tools to do the job.

Skill is the ability to perform a certain physical or mental task. An example would be a dentist's physical skill to fill a tooth without damaging the nerve or a computer programmer's ability to organise 50,000 lines of code in a logical sequential order.

Mental or cognitive skill competencies include analytic thinking (processing knowledge and data, determining cause and effect, organising data and plans) and conceptual thinking (recognising patterns in complex data).

2.1.2 Knowledge

Information accumulated in a particular area of expertise (e.g., accounting, selling, servicing, and management). "Whoever acquires knowledge but does not practice it is like one who ploughs a field but does not sow it." Knowledge is the understanding acquired through learning.

Knowledge is defined as information organised in a way that one can act on it. This implies that it has to be in context, i.e., what is knowledge to one might not be knowledge to another. By nature, knowledge is incomplete, conceptual and difficult to transfer. We gain knowledge by experience or after an interaction with someone or something like an instructor or a manual. It is the instructor's responsibility to transfer appropriate knowledge to the student, attain understanding and promote self-efficacy, or the willingness to act on the knowledge learned.

Knowledge is the information a person has in specific content areas, for example a surgeon's knowledge of nerves and muscles in the human body. Knowledge is a complex competency. Scores on knowledge tests often fail to predict work performance because they fail to measure knowledge and skills in the way they are actually used on the job. First, many knowledge tests measure rote memory, when what is important is the ability to find information. Memory of facts is less important than knowing which facts exist that is relevant to a specific problem, and where to find them when needed. Second, knowledge tests are "respondent." They measure the test takers' ability to choose which of several options is the right response, but not whether a person can act based on knowledge. For example, the ability to choose which of five items is an effective argument is very different from the ability to stand up in a conflict situation and argue persuasively. Finally, knowledge best predicts what someone can do, not what he or she will do.

2.1.3 Motive

Recurrent thought driving behaviours (e.g., drive for achievement, affiliation). A motive is an underlying need or thought pattern that drives, directs and selects an individual's behaviour, for example, need for achievement. Motivation can be negative, extrinsic or intrinsic. Even if a field service engineer has the skill, there is no guarantee of high performance. Certain internal and external factors that stimulate desire and energy in people to be continually interested and committed to the job are nothing but motives.

Motives are the things a person consistently thinks about or wants that cause action. Motives "drive, direct, and select" behaviour toward certain actions or goals and away from others. For example, motivated people consistently set challenging goals for themselves, take personal responsibility for accomplishing them, and use feedback to do better.

2.1.4 Traits

A general disposition to behave in certain ways for instance with self-confidence, self-control, flexibility and stress resistance. A trait is something about you that makes "you." Trait refers to a characteristic caused by genetics.

Traits are physical characteristics and consistent responses to situations or information. Reaction time and good eyesight are physical trait competencies of combat pilots.

Emotional self-control and initiative are more complex, "consistent responses to situations". Some people do not "blow up" at others and do act "beyond the call of duty" to solve problems under stress. These trait competencies are characteristic of successful managers.

Motives and competencies are intrinsic or self-starting "master traits" that predict what people will do on their jobs long-term, without close supervision.

2.1.5 Self-concept

The term self-concept is a general term used to refer to how people think about, evaluate or perceive themselves. To be aware of oneself is to have a concept of oneself. Baumeister (1999) provides the following *self-concept* definition: "*the individual's belief about himself or herself, including the person's attributes and who and what the self is*".

Self-concept is a person's attitudes, values, or self-image. In other words it is a person's belief that he or she can be effective in almost any situation.

A person's values are respondent or reactive motives that predict what he or she will do in the short-term and in situations where others are in charge. For example, someone who values being a leader is more likely to exhibit leadership behaviour if he or she is told a task or job will be "a test of leadership ability." People who value being "in management" but do not intrinsically like or spontaneously think about influencing others at the motive level often attain management positions but then fail.

2.2 Iceberg Model of Competency

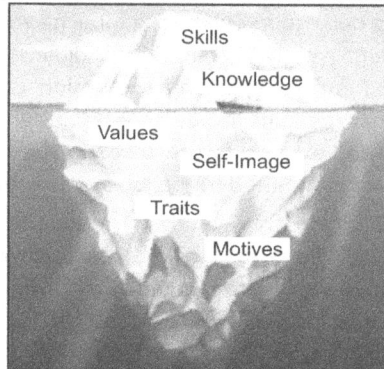

Fig. 2.1: Iceberg Model of Competency

The iceberg model for competencies takes the help of an iceberg to explain the concept of competency. An iceberg has just one-ninth of its volume above water and the rest remains beneath the surface of the sea. Similarly, a competency has some visible components like knowledge and skills, but other behavioural components like attitude, traits, thinking styles, self-image, organisational fit etc. are hidden or beneath the surface.

We can think of competencies in terms of an iceberg. Technical competencies like knowledge and skill are at the tip—above the waterline, clearly visible and easier to assess. Behavioural competencies like self-image, trait, and motive are below the waterline—more difficult to assess and often harder to develop. Behavioural competencies can be understood as manifestations of how a person views himself or herself (self-image), how he or she typically behaves (traits) or which gives purpose and direction to his behaviour (motives).

Iceberg Model: Spencer and Spencer proposed the "Iceberg Model" to divide underlying characteristics that caused behaviours and performance in a job into five categories.

1. Motives were consistent thoughts or desires that caused a particular action. They impelled behaviours toward certain actions or goals and not toward others.
    Example: Achievement motivation.

2. Traits referred to physical and mental characteristics related to the ways a person consistently responded in certain ways to situations and messages.
    Examples: Reaction time and emotional self-control.

3. Self-concept referred to an individual's attitudes, values, and self-image, including self-identity and self-confidence.

4. Knowledge referred to a body of information usually of a factual or procedural nature needed to understand a certain subject.

   Example: A surgeon's knowledge of nerves and muscles in the human body.

5. Skills referred to the ability to accomplish a certain mental task such as analytical thinking and conceptual thinking or a physical task.

   Example: A dentist filling a tooth without damaging the nerve.

According to the iceberg model, knowledge and skills were visible and appeared at the top of the iceberg, as shown in Fig. 2.1. They were relatively easily developed and improved through education and job training. On the other hand, motives and traits were more likely to be hidden since they comprise the innermost part of an individual's personality. In Fig. 2.1, motives and traits appeared at the base of the iceberg. Therefore, they were more difficult to develop and reform through school education and job training. Although the authors grouped self-concept in hidden competencies, they indicated that it could still be changed to a certain degree through constant education, consultation, and training.

2.3 Operant and Respondent Traits of Competency

Competency characteristics are usually classified as

1. Operant or respondent traits (for example, motives, self-concepts, attitudes, values, or occupational preference).

2. Declarative knowledge (for example, know that).

3. Procedural skills (for example, know how).

Procedural skills may be cognitive or behavioural skills. Content knowledge is declarative knowledge (that is, what one knows) of facts or procedures, either technical (such as how to trouble-shoot a defective computer) or interpersonal (such as the five rules of effective feedback), as measured by respondent tests. Skill is procedural knowledge (that is, what one can do), either convert (for example, deductive or inductive reasoning) or observable (for example, active listening skills in an interview).

Fig. 2.2, known as an iceberg diagram, shows the easily visible skill and knowledge competencies above the iceberg's waterline and the less easily seen self-concept and motivation traits below the iceberg's waterline.

Traits are general dispositions to attend to certain categories of stimuli or to behave or respond in certain ways, or to do both. Traits can be categorised as operant or respondent. Operant traits are intrinsic drives to act in the absence of environmental pressures or rewards. These traits are formed early in life by association of thoughts and behaviours with pleasure and they are satisfied by the intrinsic pleasure of engaging in the thought or activity itself. Respondent traits are conscious beliefs or value drives formed by early social reinforcement. These traits are satisfied by external reinforcement praise or by symbolic or monetary rewards.

The iceberg model has implications for the design of competency-based human resource application. Competencies differ in the extent to which they can be taught. Content knowledge and behavioural skills are easier to reach and attitudes and values are harder. Although it is possible to change motives and traits (McClelland and Winter, 1971), the process is lengthy, difficult and expensive. From a cost-effectiveness standpoint, the rule is to hire for core motivation and traits characteristics and develop knowledge and skill. Most organisations do the reverse. They hire on the basis of educational credentials and assume that candidates come with the appropriate motives and traits or can be indoctrinated with them. It is more cost-effective to hire people with the right motives and traits and train them in knowledge and skills needed to do specific jobs. In the words of one personnel manager, "You can teach a turkey to climb a tree, but it's easier to hire a squirrel."

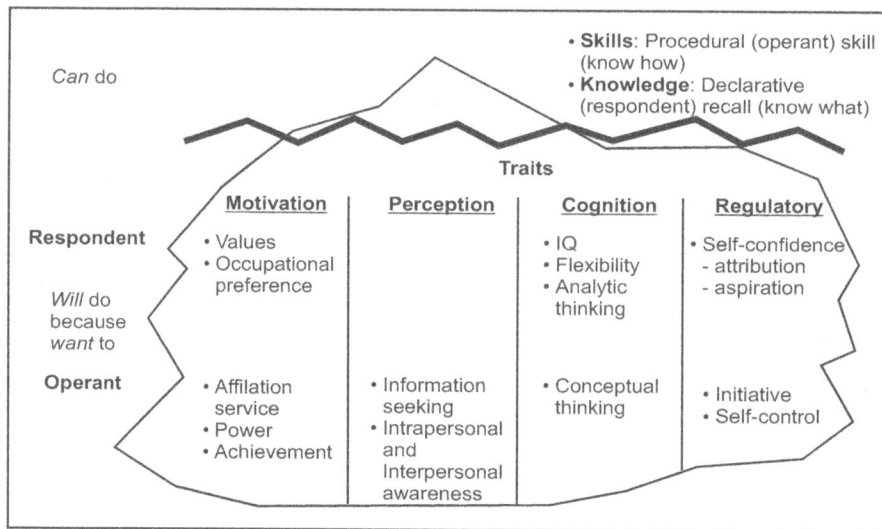

Fig. 2.2: Iceberg Levels of Competencies

The operant-respondent distinction has provided a major organising framework for the data generated through the experimental analysis of behaviour. Problems have been encountered, however, in using it as an explanatory concept for such phenomena as avoidance and conditioned suppression. Data now exist that do not fit neatly into the framework. Moreover, the discovery of auto-shaping has highlighted difficulties in isolating the two types of behaviour and conditioning. Despite these problems, the operant-respondent framework remains the most successful paradigm currently available for organising behavioural data. Research and theoretical efforts are directed to modifying the framework to account for disparate data.

2.4 Competency Models

Competency model is a framework for organising a collection of observable skills, behaviours, and attitudes that affect the quality of work people do. It describes what people need to know and be able to do in order to execute their responsibilities effectively.

Even though the definition is simple, the role of competency models in organisational design has become extremely significant. In fact, as the war for talent continues to rage, many organisations have come to view competencies as foundational to effective talent management and have classified competency models as a strategic imperative. The reason for this is that the best organisations are using competencies to

- Recruit and select employees to ensure organisational fit.
- Set performance expectations and measure contributions objectively.
- Make employees focus on what is critical to enhancing their contribution and increasing their satisfaction.
- Provide a roadmap for employee development and career planning.

In addition, by assessing "competency gaps" in relation to individuals and groups, competency models become valuable inputs to creating highly targeted training initiatives.

Competency Models – Implementing the Good Practices

When done right, competency models enable an organisation to align employees' performance with the overall business strategy. If the strategy is the "what" for the organisation, the competency model describes "how" employees should execute in order to deliver on the strategy. The impact is cumulative across the organisation – the most effective competency models are designed and implemented with the intent of raising individual performance results, and to increase the levels of proficiency throughout the enterprise.

Competency modeling helps HR functions leverage their strategic roles by vertically aligning the different HR practice areas to the organisation's strategic objectives. In addition, competency modeling helps to interconnect the various HR practices, which in turn, reinforces the integration of talent management activities.

When different HR processes are designed and implemented using a common competency framework, it results in a holistic, self-reinforcing system. For example, when an organisation selects, develops, rewards, and promotes employees on the same set of competencies, it contributes to building a strong organisational climate by establishing high performance work systems.

In terms of approach, there are various ways to drive organisational improvement, depending on organisational needs.

- A **core competency model** supports the development of those critical core competencies that are required by an organisation to achieve its defined strategy.

- A **technical/functional competency model** supports the development of technical, role-specific competencies that enable an organisation to execute more effectively.

- A **leadership competency model** supports the development of key leadership capabilities in order to build leadership impact within the organisation.

These different approaches may be combined in various ways, but regardless of the approach selected, the following success factors should be built into the framework design process. The model should be

- Limited to a set of critical competencies that align to strategic intent.
- Simple, pragmatic, and easy to use.
- Integrated with and used as the foundation for people processes.
- Systematically implemented and communicated.
- Developed, endorsed, and used by organisational leaders.

Competency Models – Avoiding the Bad and Ugly Practices

If all of this sounds desirable and straightforward, the reality is that competencies can be hard to define and understand and, for HR professionals, the task of developing and implementing a competency model can seem daunting. In addition, all too often, the work on competency model development is carried out by HR and is detached from the business. This can easily lead to models that become over-engineered and difficult to apply. It can also lead to prolonged implementation cycles that end up stalled.

Rounding the competency framework in the context of the business is essential, and there are a number of best practices that can help to avoid the "bad" and the "ugly" practices of competency modeling.

- **Brand competency modeling as a strategic initiative:** Avoid positioning competency model projects as HR activities. Instead, market them as strategic imperatives that are necessary for helping the organisation achieve its business outcomes.

- **Align competencies to the organisation's values and strategy:** Enlist senior executives to help you identify critical competencies necessary to perpetuate the culture and execute the strategy of the organisation.

- **Identify critical (or differentiating) competencies:** Avoid exhaustive lists of competencies and keep models manageable. Select ten or fewer core competencies to create organisational focus and another five to fifteen competencies to address the skills that make a real difference for different jobs.

- **Start with off-the-shelf models and research, but do not over-rely on them:** Leverage existing models and research as starting points to accelerate model development, but recognise the need to customise models to best align with your organisation's specific strategy and minimise the risk of diluting the model's impact.

- **Engage key business stakeholders in development:** Conduct focus groups and review sessions with key business stakeholders to improve the accuracy and quality of the model, while building consensus in the process.

- **Integrate competency models with people processes:** Ensure competency visibility by explicitly integrating competencies into existing people processes to improve adoption and business impact. To avoid implementing more than the organisation can absorb, focus on the areas of biggest impact as a way to gain traction and build initial adoption.

- **Determine how you will measure success:** Be clear and explicit about the business impact you want to achieve, and identify appropriate metrics for measuring it.

- **Communicate from the top:** Use senior leadership to set expectations with employees regarding how competencies will be used both short-term and long-term and encourage them to model the behaviours that they want the rest of the organisation to adopt.

Competency Models – High on the HR Action Agenda

Competency models are now a critical component for any organisation that wants to flourish in this uncertain economy. Competency modeling can no longer be viewed as an HR "task" and must be viewed instead as an organisational game changer. The responsibility to make this case rests with HR.

- HR professionals must be comfortable engaging executives in relevant business dialogue about talent and the importance of competency modeling in building a foundation for strategic people-related practices that support finding, keeping, and growing the talent.

- HR can no longer stand at a distance from the business. It must be at its centre advocating the comprehensive talent agenda and demonstrating how competency models enable strategic and integrated HR talent management.

Research shows that strategic and integrated talent management practices are directly linked to increased shareholder value.

By positioning competency models as a business solution, executives may just realise that competency models are not as ugly as they were once thought to be. After the competency framework is properly implemented, and the operational benefits begin to accrue, those business executives may come to believe that they thought of it themselves.

Competency model is a collection of **competencies** that together define successful performance in a particular work setting. **Competency models** are the foundation for important human resource functions such as recruitment and hiring, training and development, and performance management.

2.5 Leadership and Managerial Competency Models

The leadership competency model incorporates four broad areas.

1. **Leadership**: Applies leadership competencies to successfully execute strategy.

2. **Business Knowledge/Organisational Acumen**: Applies resources, customer needs, and processes to make sound strategic and business decisions.

3. **Builds Relationships/Communication**: Cultivates effective relationships to create a culture that supports the department, and organisation goals and strategy.

4. **Self-Management and Development**: On-going development of skills and competencies to lead the division and its strategies.

This competency model is divided into three main groups.

- Core Competencies
- Leadership Competencies
- Professional Competencies

These three groups of competencies are considered the **Pyramid of Leadership**, which collectively form the basic requirements for becoming a leader.

The diagram below shows the Pyramid of Leadership, while the table below it explains each level in more detail.

Adult Learning
Instructional Design
Rapid design
Consulting
Instruction

Professional
Competencies
(for instructional
Designers)

Leadership Abilities
Visioning Process
Create and Lead Teams
Assess Situations Quickly and Accurately
Foster Conflict Resolutions (win-win)
Project Management
Implement Employee Involvement Strategies
Coach and Train
Peers and Subordinates

Leadership
Competencies

Core Competencies

Communication Teamwork
Creative Problem Solving
Interpersonal Skills
Manage Client relationships
Self-Direction
Flexibility
Professionalism
Financial
Business Acumen

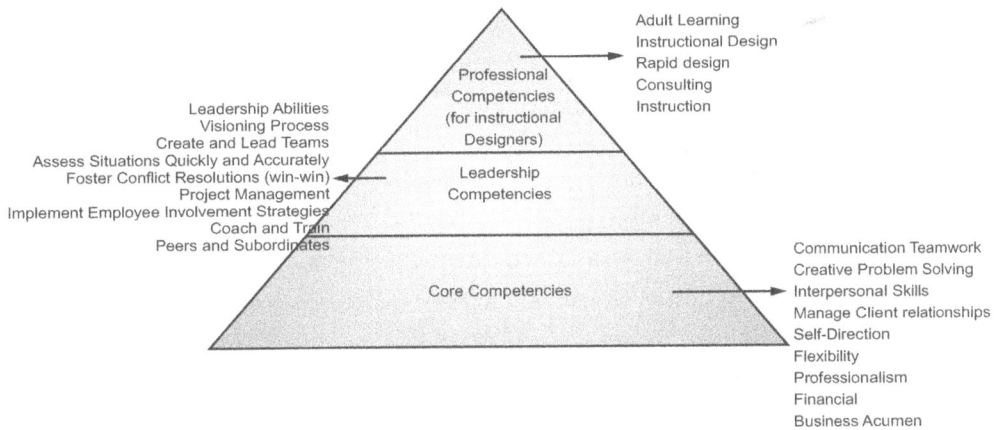

Fig. 2.3: Leadership and Managerial Competency Model

2.5.1 Core Competencies

These are the personal skills required at all levels of leadership. Essential competencies provide the foundation that a person needs to become a leader. Without a strong foundation, the sides of the pyramid will soon crumble and fall as the base gives away.

1. **Communicating**
   Basic Communications
   o Express oneself effectively both orally and in written form.
   o Communicate plans and activities in a manner that supports strategies for employee involvement.
   o Actively listen to others.
   Negotiating
   o Skillfully settle differences by using a win-win approach in order to maintain relationships.

2. **Teamwork**
   o Use appropriate interpersonal style to steer team members towards the goal.
   o Allocate decision-making and other responsibilities to the appropriate individuals.
   o Organize resources to accomplish tasks with maximum efficiency.
   o Influence events to achieve goals beyond what was called for.

3. **Creative Problem Solving**
   o Identify and collect information relevant to the problem.
   o Use brainstorming techniques to create a variety of choices.
   o Select the best course of action by identifying all the alternatives and then make a logical assumption.

4. **Interpersonal Skills**

   o Treat others with respect, trust, and dignity.

   o Work well with others by being considerate of the needs and feelings of each individual.

   o Promote a productive culture by valuing individuals and their contributions.

5. **Manage Client Relationships**

   o Work effectively with both internal and external customers.

   o Gather and analyse customer feedback to assist in decision-making.

6. **Self-direction**

   o Establish goals, deliverables, timelines, and budgets with little or no motivation from superiors (self-motivation rather than passive acceptance).

   o Assemble and lead teams to achieve established goals within deadlines.

7. **Flexibility**

   o Be willing to change to meet organisational needs.

   o Challenge established norms and make hard, but correct decisions.

   o Adapt to stressful situations.

8. **Build appropriate relationships**

   o Network with peers and associates to build a support base.

   o Build constructive and supportive relationships.

9. **Professionalism**

   o Set the example.

   o Stay current in terms of professional development.

   o Contribute to and promote the development of the profession through active participation in the community.

10. **Financial**

    o Do not waste resources.

    o Look for methods to improve processes that have a positive impact on the bottom line.

11. **Business Acumen**

    o React positively to key developments in area of expertise that may affect the business.

    o Lead process improvement programs in all major systems falling under area of control.

2.5.2 Leadership Competencies

These are the skills needed to drive the organisation onto the cutting edge of new technologies. Leadership competencies form the basic structure that separates leaders from bosses. These skills create the walls and interiors of the pyramid. Without them, a leader is just a hollow windbag, or as Scott Adams of Dilbert fame best characterises it, "a pointy-head boss."

1. **Leadership Abilities**

   o Display attributes that make people glad to follow.

   o Provide a feeling of trust.

   o Rally the troops and build morale when the going gets tough.

2. **Visioning Process**

   o Apply effort to increase productiveness in areas needing the most improvement.

   o Create and set goals (visions).

   o Sense the environment by using personal sway to influence subordinates and peers.

   o Gain commitment by influencing the team to set objectives and buy in on the process.

   o Reinforce change by embracing it (prevent relapse into prior state).

3. **Create and Lead Teams**

   o Develop high-performance teams by establishing a spirit of cooperation and cohesion for achieving goals.

   o Quickly take teams out of the storming phase and into the performing phase.

4. **Assess Situations Quickly and Accurately**

   o Take charge when the situation demands it.

   o Make the right things happen on time.

5. **Foster Conflict Resolutions (win-win)**

   o Effectively handle disagreements and conflicts.

   o Settle disputes by focusing on solving the problems, without offending egos.

   o Provide support and expertise to other leaders with respect to managing people.

   o Evaluate the feasibility of alternative dispute resolution mechanisms.

6. **Project Management**

   o Track critical steps in projects to ensure they are completed on time.

   o Identify and react to the outside forces that might influence or alter the organisation's goals.

- Establish a course of action to accomplish a specific goal.
- Identify, evaluate and implement measurement systems for current and future projects.

7. Implement Employee Involvement Strategies

- Develop ownership by bringing employees in on the decision-making and planning process.
- Provide the means to enable employee success, while maintaining the well-being of the organisation.
- Develop processes to engage employees in achieving the objectives of the organisation.
- Empower employees by giving them the authority to get things accomplished in the most efficient and timely manner.

8. Coach and Train Peers and Subordinates

- Recognise that learning happens at every opportunity (treat mistakes as a learning event).
- Develop future leaders by being involved in the company's mentoring program.
- Provide performance feedback, coaching, and career development to teams and individuals to maximise their probability of success.
- Ensure leadership at every level by coaching employees to ensure the right things happen.
- Ensure performance feedback is an integral part of the day-to-day activities.

2.5.3 Professional Competencies for Learning/Training Leaders

These are the skills and knowledge needed to direct the systems and processes that a leader controls. Professional competencies form the mortar that binds the pyramid together. Without some knowledge of the technical skills that they direct, the pyramid soon begins to fall apart and the organisation begins to operate in a damage control mode.

Each organisation requires a different set of professional competencies for each leadership position. Although leaders do not need to be Subject Matter Experts (SME) for the tasks that they direct, they must have a basic understanding of the systems and processes that they control. Again, each position requires a different set of skills and knowledge.

1. Adult Learning

- Understand and appreciate the diverse experiences of learners.
- Facilitate self-direction and help with the informal learning of others.

2. **Instructional Design**

   o Use the Instructional Design (ISD) model.

   o Conduct needs assessment and analyse performance needs.

   o Design for maximum performance.

   o Develop material by fleshing out design.

   o Deliver (implement) learning package.

   o Evaluate using formative and summative methods throughout the entire process.

3. **Rapid Design**

   o Use prototypes to quickly create and deliver learning packages.

4. **Consulting**

   o Determine stakeholder's needs.

   o Negotiate a solution.

   o Ensure solution fulfills a business and/or organisation requirement.

5. **Instruction**

   o Plan and prepare for instruction.

   o Engage learners throughout the entire instruction.

   o Demonstrate effective presentation and facilitation skills.

   o Provide clarification and feedback.

   o Provide retention and transfer of newly learned skills and knowledge.

2.6 Organisational Change

Organisational change may be apparent when there is a gap between how the work area is operating and how it should be operating to ensure successful future growth, Organisational change may be a result of the work area identifying goals that they want to achieve.

Change Management

Change management is a structured approach to shifting individuals, teams and organisations from a current state to a desired future state. It is an organisational process aimed at helping employees to accept and embrace changes in their current business environment.

Kotler defines change management as the utilisation of basic structures and tools to control any organisational change effort.

Resistance to Change

One of the most well documented facts from studies of individual and organisational behaviour is that organisations and their members resist change. Resistance to change can be a source of functional conflict. For example, resistance to a change in a product line can stimulate a healthy debate over the merits of the idea and result in a better decision. However, there is a definite negative side to resistance to change that it hinders adaptation and progress.

Resistance to change does not necessarily surface in standardised ways. Resistance can be overt, implicit, immediate or deferred. It is easier for the management to deal with resistance when it is overt and immediate.

The greater challenge is managing resistance that is implicit or deferred. Implicit resistance efforts are more subtle – loss of loyalty to the organisation, loss of motivation to work, increased errors or mistakes, increased absenteeism and hence more difficult to recognise.

Let us look at the sources of resistance. For analytical purposes, we have categorised them by individual and organisational sources. In the real world, the sources often overlap.

Individual Resistance

Fig. 2.4 depicts five reasons why individuals may resist change.

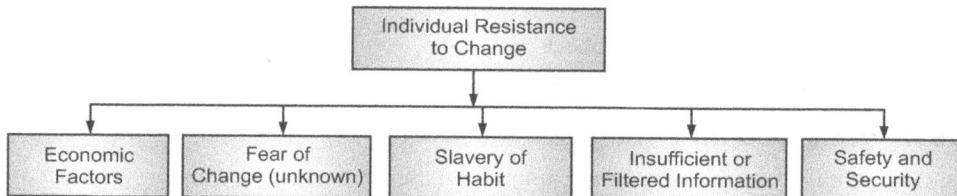

Fig. 2.4: Causes of Individual Resistance

1. **Habit:** A human being is a slave to his/her habit. Life is complex enough and to cope with this complexity, humans rely on habits or programmed responses. When confronted with change, this tendency to respond in our accustomed ways becomes a source of resistance. So when one's department is moved to a new building, it means one is likely to have to change many habits adjusting to the new office location and layout and certain schedule adjustments.

2. **Security:** Safety and security are a very basic human need. People with the need for security are likely to resist change, because it threatens their feelings of safety. Thus, there is a resistance to a change in the nature of job.

3. **Economic factors:** Changes in job or established work routines can also arouse economic phobias. People are concerned that their previous productivity and quality levels may be affected; and so would their pay, which is linked to productivity.

4. **Fear of the unknown:** Changes substitute ambiguity and uncertainty for the known. Employees in organisations dislike uncertainty, for example, with the introduction of TQM production workers will have to learn statistical process control techniques. They may therefore develop a negative attitude towards TQM if required to learn statistical techniques.

5. **Selective information processing:** Individuals shape their world through their perceptions. Hence, individuals are guilty of selectively processing information. In order to keep their perceptions intact, they hear what they want to hear, they ignore information that challenges the world they have created.

Organisational Resistance

Hall has discussed the theory of resistance to change by organisations. Organisations by their very nature are conservative. They actively resist change. One does not have to look far to see evidence of this phenomenon. Government agencies want to continue doing what they have been doing for years.

Six major sources of organisational resistance are shown in Fig. 2.5

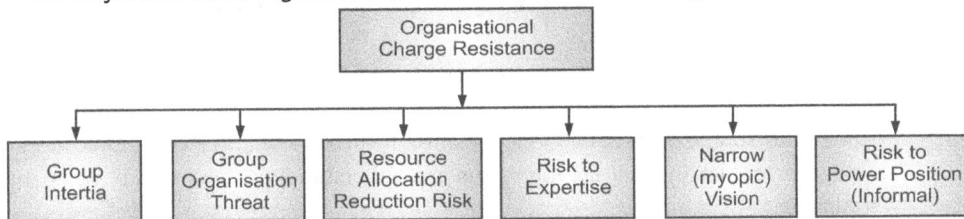

Fig. 2.5: Causes of Groups Resistance to Change

1. **Structural inertia:** Organisations have built-in mechanisms to produce stability. For example, the selection process systematically selects certain people and role requirements and skills formalisation provides job descriptions, rules and procedures for employees to follow. The people who are hired into an organisation are chosen for fit. They are then shaped and directed to behave in certain ways. When an organisation is confronted with change this structural inertia acts as a counter balance to sustain stability.

2. **Limited focus of change:** Organisations are made up of a number of interdependent subsystems. One cannot change one without affecting the other. For example, if management changes the technological processes without simultaneously modifying the organisation's structure to match the change in technology, this change is not likely to be accepted.

3. **Group inertia:** Even if individuals want to change their behavior, group norms may act as a constraint on individual union members. If union norms dictate resisting any change made by management, the member is likely to resist.

4. **Threat to expertise:** Changes in organisational patterns may threaten the expertise of specialised groups. The introduction of decentralised personal computers, which allow managers to gain access to information directly from a company's mainframe, is an example of a change that was strongly resisted by many information systems departments in the early 1980s. It was a threat to the specialised skills of those in the centralised systems departments.

5. **Threat to established power relationships:** Any redistribution of decision-making authority can threaten long established power relationships within the work teams. In time, this kind of change is perceived as threatening by supervisors and middle managers.

6. **Threat to established resource allocations:** Those groups in the organisation that control sizable resources often see change as a threat.

Overcoming Resistance to Change

Kotter has suggested six tactics for use by change agents in dealing with resistance to change.

1. **Education and communication:** Resistance can be reduced through communication with employees to help them see the logic of a change. This tactic basically assumes the source of resistance lies in misinformation or poor communication. If employees receive the full facts and get misunderstandings cleared up, resistance will subside.

2. **Participation:** It is difficult for individuals to resist a change decision in which they participated. Prior to making a change, those opposed to it can be brought into the decision process.

3. **Facilitation and support:** Change agents can offer a range of supportive efforts to reduce resistance. When employee fear and anxiety is high, employee counselling and new skills training can be imparted.

4. **Negotiation:** If the resistance is centred in a few powerful individuals a specific reward package can be negotiated that will meet their individual needs. Negotiation as a tactic may be necessary, when resistance comes from a powerful source. There is the risk that once the change agent negotiates with one party to avoid resistance, he is open to the possibility of being pressurised by other individuals in positions of power.

5. **Co-option:** Co-option is a form of both manipulation and participation. It seeks to buy off the leaders of a resistance group by giving them key roles in the change decision. The leader's advice is not to seek a better decision but to get their endorsement.

6. **Coercion:** Last on the list of tactics is coercion. It is the application of direct threats or force upon the resisters. Examples of coercion are threats of transfer, loss of promotions, negative evaluation and poor letters of recommendation. The advantages and drawbacks of coercion are approximately the same as those mentioned for manipulation and co-optation.

2.7 Delphi Technique

Adler and Ziglio describe the Delphi method as an exercise in group communication among a panel of geographically dispersed experts. These experts share a common interest (the subject of the Delphi), but usually represent different points of view.

The original Delphi process consisted of three key elements: a structured information flow, feedback to the participants, and anonymity for the participants. Fowles describes the following ten steps for the Delphi method.

1. Formation of a team to undertake and monitor a Delphi on a given subject.

2. Selection of one or more panels to participate in the exercise.

3. Development of the first round Delphi questionnaire.

4. Testing the questionnaire for proper wording, ambiguities, and vagueness.

5. Transmission of the first round questionnaires to the panelists.

6. Analysis of the first round responses.

7. Preparation of the second round questionnaires (and possible testing).

8. Transmission of the second round questionnaires to the panelists.

9. Analysis of the second round responses (steps 7 to 9 are reiterated as long as desired or necessary to achieve stability in the results).

10. Preparation of a report to present the conclusions of the exercise.

Each round poses a series of Likert questions, the answers are tabulated, and the results are used to form the basis for the next round of questions. Through several iterations, usually three, this process synthesises the experts' responses, resulting in a consensus that reflects the group's intuition, perceptive, and expert knowledge. Although the outcome of a Delphi sequence is nothing but opinion, they are the opinions of the experts who made up the panel and the panel viewpoint is summarised statistically rather than in terms of a majority vote.

Participant Selection

Participant selection for a Delphi forecasting study is critical. Experts should be identified and a nomination process used to select participants. Random selection is not acceptable. The researcher needs to locate and target individuals who have the knowledge and experience in the subject at hand, and are self-motivated. These participants remain anonymous to each other to facilitate the free expression of ideas without bias.

According to **Ludwig**, the majority of Delphi studies used are between fifteen to twenty respondents, but Dalkey, Rourke, Lewis and Snyder reported there was a definite and monolithic increase in the reliability of group responses with increasing group size. They reported reliability, with a correlation coefficient approaching .9, with a group size of thirteen. Experiments by Brockhoff, however, suggest that under ideal circumstances, groups as small as four can perform well.

Instrument Development and Data Collection

In a Delphi study, developing and processing questionnaires are interconnected.

Participants agree to receive and respond to a series of questionnaires; usually three are needed. The first questionnaire could take several forms, but would most likely be one or two open-ended questions related to the subject. The second questionnaire is a culmination of information collected from the first questionnaire consisting of a series of structured questions developed by the researcher. Participants rank-order items or use a Likert-type rating scale to prioritise items, and are asked to comment on their rationale and add additional items. The third questionnaire (and any subsequent questionnaires) asks participants to re-rate each item, but this time, they are provided with (a) statistical feedback regarding their own ratings, (b) feedback on how the group rated the same item, and (c) a summary of comments made by participants.

This process continues until a predetermined level of consensus is reached or no new information is gained, but Altschuld found that three iterations were usually sufficient as not enough new information was gained to warrant the cost of more iteration.

2.8 360-degree Feedback

360-degree Feedback is a system or process in which employees receive confidential, anonymous feedback from the people who work around them. This typically includes the employee's manager, peers, and direct reports. A mixture of about eight to twelve people fill out an anonymous online feedback form that asks questions covering a broad range of workplace competencies. The feedback forms include questions that are measured on a rating scale, and ask raters to provide written comments. The person receiving feedback also fills out a self-rating survey that includes the same survey questions that others receive in their forms.

Managers and leaders within organisations use 360 feedback surveys to get a better understanding of their strengths and weaknesses. The 360-feedback system automatically tabulates the results and presents those in a format that helps the feedback recipient create a development plan. Individual responses are usually combined with responses from other people in the same rater category (e.g. peer, direct report) in order to preserve anonymity and to give the employee a clear picture of his/her greatest overall strengths and weaknesses.

360-feedback can also be a useful development tool for people who are not in a management role. Strictly speaking, a "non-manager" 360 assessment is not measuring feedback from 360-degrees since there are no direct reports, but the same principles still apply. 360 Feedback for non-managers is useful to help people be more effective in their current roles and to help them understand what areas they should focus on if they want to move into a management role.

How is a 360-degree Feedback used?

Companies typically use a 360-feedback system in one of two ways.

1. **360 Feedback as a Development Tool to help employees recognise strengths and weaknesses and become more effective.**

When done properly, 360 is highly effective as a development tool. The feedback process gives people an opportunity to provide unknown feedback to a co-worker that they might otherwise be uncomfortable giving. Feedback recipients gain insight into how others perceive them and have an opportunity to adjust behaviours and develop skills that will enable them to excel at their jobs.

2. **360-feedback as a Performance Appraisal Tool to measure employee performance.**

Using a 360-degree feedback system for performance appraisal is a common practice, but not always a good idea. It is difficult to properly structure a 360-feedback process that creates an atmosphere of trust when you use 360 evaluations to measure performance. Moreover, 360-feedback focuses on behaviours and competencies more than on basic skills, job requirements, and performance objectives. These aspects are most appropriately addressed by an employee and his/her manager as part of an annual review and performance appraisal process. It is certainly possible and can be beneficial to incorporate 360 feedback into a larger performance management process, but only with clear communication on how the 360-feedback will be used.

2.9 HR Generic Competency Model

As the interest in measuring and predicting performance in the workplace has grown tremendously, the term "competency" appears to have become a staple part of an HR practitioner's vocabulary. While it is among the most frequently used terms among the HR practitioners, it is also one of the least understood. **Selznick** first brought about the concept of "competency", and McClelland thereafter used the term to illustrate the major key factor to affect individual learning. The term "competency" has been defined in the academic literature from several different points of view. It was popularised in the management field through the work of Boyatzis. Human resource managers view the concept as a technical tool to implement strategic direction through the tactics of recruitment, placement, training, assessment, promotion, rewards, and personnel planning. **Strebler** asserts that the term has no widely accepted single definition. Competencies may be "expressed as behaviours that an individual needs to demonstrate," or they may be "expressed as minimum standards of performance". The term competency" has been used to refer to the meaning expressed as behaviours, while the term "competences" has been used to refer to the meaning expressed as "standards." Organisations in the private sector tend to use the term "competency model," while those in the public sector use "competence model".

A review of the literature shows three main positions taken towards the definition of the term. Competencies are defined as observable performance, the standard or quality of the outcome of the person's performance, or the underlying attributes of a person. **Boyatzis** defines competency as an "underlying characteristic of a person which results in effective and/or superior performance in a job." Boyatzis expands the definition to include "a motive, trait, skill, and aspect of one's self-image or social role, or a body of knowledge which he/she uses." Hager defines competency as "the specification of knowledge and skills and the application of that knowledge and skills to the standard of performance required." A well-accepted definition of competency refers to the underlying attributes of a person such as their knowledge, skills, or abilities. The use of this definition creates a focus on the required inputs of individuals in order for them to produce competent performances. This means that the individuals must have prerequisite knowledge in order to perform competently.

Kanungo, Misra and **Parry** assert the term "skills" as task centred and it is best suited for routine or programmed tasks. **Grzeda** states that there is some evidence to indicate that knowledge and competency are synonymous terms. In the managerial competence literature, "knowledge" is often considered in relation to business school curriculum content and knowledge-based competencies are understood as knowledge of subject matter, ranging from the more specific and concrete, to the broader, more general or more abstract. Spector further defines knowledge, skills, abilities, and other characteristics (KSAOs). "Knowledge" is what a person knows that is relevant to the job.

"Skill" is what a person is able to do on the job. "Ability" (mental, physical, and psychomotor) is the capacity to learn a skill, and "other characteristics" include attitudes, beliefs, personality characteristics, temperaments, and values.

Järvalt recognises the importance of the competency approach as it supports the strategic and integrated approach to developing strategic leadership. Although there are many ways of defining competencies, the approach of defining it as "an underlying characteristic of an employee which results in effective and/or superior performance in a job" is broadly accepted. Järvalt stresses the importance of a competency framework or a model that provides a measurement instrument by which competencies can be expressed and assessed.

Competency models are created to illustrate how competencies lead to performance. The models illustrate personal and job-related characteristics, the organisational context, and the interrelationship of those elements that result in performance in relation to the predetermined standards. Organisations generally use competency models for various purposes, and the general reasons that remain valid across all users as given by Palan are (a) to provide a way in which the concept of competency can be applied to organisational needs and (b) understand the variables determining performance and their correlation to it and enable the rapid deployment of competencies for use in an organisation. The construct of the model in terms of components as well as data collection and analysis techniques will depend on the planned use. However according to Palan, the model may define core requirements for all employees regardless of function or level; define requirements only for specific levels/functions and define requirements for each distinct role or job in an organisation. Cooper defines a competency model as "collection of competencies and standards of performance establishing qualifications for a specific job position."

According to **Lucia** and **Lepsinger**, a competency model is "a descriptive tool that identifies the skills, knowledge, and personal characteristics as well as behaviours, needed to perform a role effectively in an organisation, and to help the business meet its strategic objectives." A competency model can be used to clarify jobs and work expectations, hire the best available people, maximise productivity, enhance the 360-degree feedback process, adapt to change, and align behaviours with organisational strategies and values. Competency models identify the competencies that truly have an impact on results or deliverables. Not only are there many definitions of "competency" found in literature, there are also various approaches used in framing and understanding competencies. McLagan identifies six approaches that can be used to defining and developing models of competency and these are job tasks, results of work effort, outputs, knowledge, skills and attitude (KSA), qualities of superior performances, and bundles of attributes.

Draganidis and **Mentzas** define a competency model as "a list of competencies which are derived from observing satisfactory or exceptional employee performance for a specific occupation. It provides identification of the competencies employees need to develop in order to improve performance in current job or to prepare for other jobs." The late 1980s and early 1990s witnessed attempts to identify, define and draw up frameworks of key workplace competencies in Britain, Australia, and the USA. Development efforts in those countries were driven by similar concerns with the implications of workplace change and the consequent need to ensure the supply of essential generic skills that employers required. The interest on generic skills needed at the workplace is possibly due to the emergence of an information society and knowledge-based new economy. Generic skills are defined as "those transferable skills, essential for employability which is relevant at different levels for most".

The United Nation's Secretariat developed a competency model for the United Nations that adopts a broad approach that includes core competencies, core values, and managerial competencies. This is given in Figure 5. The United Nations Competency Model illustrates how progressive organisations are adopting a broad approach to generic skills that links core competencies and values with management competencies, and attributes that are required to give effect to the generic skills, and values in a high performance workplace.

2.10 Supervisory Generic Competency Model

There are twelve competencies in the competency model. These twelve competencies fall into three categories or domains. Job analysis interviews and focus group meetings were conducted to identify the knowledge and behaviours that are important to successful performance in supervisory roles.

Based on the data gathered from these interviews and focus groups, the data was consolidated into a potential list of competencies. This list was then developed into a survey, which was then completed by employees, supervisors, and managers. This step was designed to confirm the list of competencies as well as identify the most important key behaviours that define effective demonstration of each competency.

Since the Supervisory Competency Model is the foundation of the supervisory curriculum, it is important to understand the terminology so that one shares a clear understanding of what one means when one uses terms such as domain, competency, and key behaviours.

There are twelve competencies in the model that are grouped into three domains. The three domains are Interpersonal Skills, Leadership Skills, and Managerial/Supervisory Skills.

Each domain consists of a grouping of three to five competencies. The competency "Building Positive Working Relationships," for example, is part of the "Interpersonal Skills" domain.

Each competency is further defined in behavioural terms. These key behaviours define more specifically what you would see a person doing if he or she demonstrated the competency.

For example, using the competency "Building Positive Working Relationships," the competency is broadly defined as "developing and using collaborative relationships with internal and external partners and customers to facilitate the accomplishment of work goals." What does this mean behaviourally? If this competency was strength for someone, what would one see the person doing on the job? What behaviours or key actions would the person demonstrate?

For this competency, specific behavioural examples keep people within and outside the department updated and informed in a timely manner, maintain a positive attitude, and cooperate with others to pursue mutual goals.

The model is designed to give you specific examples of effective supervisory behaviours.

(A) INTERPERSONAL SKILLS

1. **Building Positive Working Relationships:** Developing and using collaborative relationships with internal and external partners and customers to facilitate the accomplishment of work goals.

Key Behaviours:

o   Keeps people within and outside the department updated and informed in a timely manner.

o   Values others' knowledge and expertise; invites the input and feedback of others; fully considers others' explanations/points of view.

o   Acknowledges requests from others promptly; is available and responsive; shows up on time for meetings and appointments.

o   Maintains a positive attitude.

o   Initiates open and candid relationships with people at all levels.

o   Interacts effectively with own and higher managers; builds solid relationship with boss.

o   Cooperates with others to pursue mutual goals.

2. **Building Trust:** Interacting with everyone in a way that gives them confidence in one's intentions and those of the organisation; fostering an environment that is fair and open to new ideas.

Key Behaviours:

o   Builds trust by being reliable and dependable; follows through on commitments.

o   Gives credit where credit is due.

o   Treats people fairly and with respect.

- Applies policies and procedures consistently when dealing with employee issues.
- Expresses consistent point of view to different audiences.
- Supports employees' decisions.
- Is honest and straightforward with others; maintains confidentiality and high personal ethical standards.
- Communicates rationale for decisions/actions; admits ineffective decisions.

3. **Communication Skills:** Clearly conveying information and ideas through a variety of media to others in formal and informal settings in a manner that engages them and helps them understand and retain the message.

Key Behaviours:

- Organises thoughts before speaking and concentrates on key points; communicates clearly and articulately; speaks concisely and to the point.
- Uses examples to clarify a point.
- Says what is on his or her mind in a direct but tactful manner.
- Adapts communication style and presentation focus to fit the audience; uses appropriate language to set the proper "tone" of the communication.
- Writes correspondence that is professional, accurate, and grammatically correct.
- Asks questions to encourage others to elaborate on their thoughts; listens carefully to input without interrupting; clarifies what others say to ensure understanding.
- Conducts effective and productive meetings (one-on-one, team, etc.) on a regular basis.
- Uses multiple modes to communicate messages.

(B) LEADERSHIP SKILLS

4. **Identifying and Mobilising Resources:** Supervising appropriate staff and resources consistent with organisational goals.

Key Behaviours:

- Identifies resources needed for work projects; is aware of available resources, both internally and externally; effectively uses all resources allocated to the area.
- Provides staff with tools, resources, and materials necessary to meet the goals of the department; knows how to access funds to meet departmental goals.
- Knows strengths and weaknesses of each employee; understands each employee's skill set.

- o Balances the workload of staff; does not constantly overload best employees.
- o Fosters cooperation among team members; focuses the team on accomplishing shared goals.
- o Leverages expertise (e.g., contacts HR for HR issues, uses Purchase for purchasing needs).
- o Resolves conflicting demands for limited resources.

5. **Initiating Action:** Taking timely action when appropriate to accomplish objectives; takes appropriate action to achieve goals; anticipates issues and takes action to address them.

Key Behaviours:

- o Foresees problems and proactively works to disarm them.
- o Anticipates future work and identifies implications.
- o Seeks new and creative ways of doing things; fosters continuous improvement.
- o Abandons past practices when new practices meet the needs of the organisation in a better way.
- o Is determined to achieve objectives; is resourceful in overcoming obstacles; shows persistence.

6. **Managing Conflict:** Dealing effectively with others in an antagonistic situation; using appropriate interpersonal styles and methods to reduce tension or conflict between two or more people.

Key Behaviours:

- o Recognises conflict and deals with it before it escalates; does not ignore or avoid issues.
- o Brings all parties together as soon as possible to discuss the issue; helps others understand all perspectives of those involved in the conflict.
- o Diffuses the situation; addresses the issue calmly; reduces others' tensions; deals effectively with irate people including customers, coworkers, and staff; expresses disagreement tactfully without letting it affect working relationships.
- o Focuses all parties on the problem and specific behaviours.
- o Focuses on the goals of the department and communicates how the conflict is impeding those goals.
- o Handles conflict situations consistently.
- o Summarises and documents what the parties agreed to do to resolve the issue.
- o Monitors the situation to ensure the conflict is resolved effectively.
- o Knows when to step in and take charge and when to provide guidance for others to resolve the issue on their own.

7. **Work Standards:** Setting appropriate standards of performance for self and others, assuming responsibility and accountability for successfully completing assignments or tasks.

Key Behaviours:

o Leads by example; expects same work standards of self as expects from staff.

o Sets clear, specific expectations up front; ensures all employees understand the expectations; maintains high standards of quality and productivity for the group.

o Develops systems and measures to ensure adherence to established standards, and ensures deviations from standards are caught early in the process.

o Evaluates project success and analyses what is to be done differently going forward.

o Ensures policies and procedures are effective and makes suggested changes to upper management.

o Strives to understand and fulfill the needs and expectations of internal and/or external customers.

o Is aware of the impact of work standards (meeting or not meeting) on other areas (internal and/or external).

o Clarifies how own department fits with organisation's direction; links group objectives/goals to broader organisational goals.

8. **Change Management:** Embracing change and acting as a change agent within the organisation to facilitate the effective implementation of change initiatives, and fostering innovative approaches to improvements in the workplace.

Key Behaviours:

o Embraces change; supports the change; takes a positive attitude toward change.

o Communicates clearly the reasons behind the change along with the advantages of the change, and its impact on the big picture.

o Acknowledges employees' fears and anxieties regarding change and helps employees through them.

o Uses data to explain and support the needed changes.

(C) MANAGERIAL/SUPERVISORY SKILLS

9. **Decision-making:** Identifying and understanding issues, problems, and opportunities; comparing data from different sources to draw conclusions; using effective approaches and facilitating others in choosing a course of action or developing appropriate solutions; taking appropriate action that is consistent with available facts, constraints, and probable consequences.

Key Behaviours:

o   Considers the importance of the decision in determining how deeply to go into information gathering and data analysis; realises when too much time (or not enough) is being spent on an issue.

o   Gathers all the needed facts to make an informed decision to avoid hasty, haphazard decisions; identifies the root cause(s) of problems.

o   Involves those impacted by the decision in the decision-making process.

o   Communicates the rationale behind decisions.

o   Empowers employees to make decisions on their own.

o   Considers the consequences and impact of decisions; assesses cost and benefit tradeoffs of different options.

o   Uses an understanding of broader organisational issues to improve decision-making.

o   Makes decisions and takes action; implements decisions; makes tough decisions when necessary.

o   Accepts accountability for decisions.

10. Planning and Organizing: Establishing courses of action to ensure that work is completed efficiently.

Key Behaviours:

o   Understands the timeframe available and creates a plan to work within and meet the established timeline.

o   Understands the relationships and dependencies between parts of a project; takes the schedules and priorities of others into account when planning projects.

o   Seeks input from others when developing a plan.

o   Translates broad goals into action plans; establishes both short and long-term goals to meet department objectives.

o   Keeps track of numerous projects and tasks at the same time; utilises planning tools; has a system for planning and organising own tasks and those of others.

o   Ensures the plan is being followed and the project is on track.

o   Establishes priorities; does not place the same importance on every task; spends time on high value tasks that drive the department's goals.

o   Has an organized workspace; is able to locate needed information easily.

Points to Remember

- **Competencies** are defined as "skills and abilities, described in behavioural terms that are coachable, observable, measurable and critical to successful individual or organisation performance", while goals are the "what" of performance, and competencies are the "how" of performance.
- Components of Competency
    1. Skills
    2. Knowledge
    3. Motive
    4. Traits
    5. Self-concept
- **A skill** is the learned capacity to carry out pre-determined consequences. Skills are learned capabilities to bring about the result you want, with maximum certainty and efficiency. Skill is defined as the ability coming from knowledge, to do something well.
- **Knowledge** is defined as information organised in a way that one can act on it. This implies that it has to be in context, i.e., what is knowledge to one might not be knowledge to another.
- **A motive** is an underlying need or thought pattern that drives, directs and selects an individual's behaviour, for example, need for achievement.
- **Traits** are physical characteristics and consistent responses to situations or information. Reaction time and good eyesight are physical trait competencies of combat pilots.
- **Self-concept** is a person's attitudes, values, or self-image. In other words it is a person's belief that he or she can be effective in almost any situation.
- The iceberg model for competencies takes the help of an iceberg to explain the concept of competency. Technical competencies like knowledge and skill are at the tip—above the waterline, clearly visible and easier to assess. Behavioural competencies like self-image, trait, and motive are below the waterline—more difficult to assess and often harder to develop.
- Competency characteristics are usually classified as
    1. Operant or respondent traits (for example, motives, self-concepts, attitudes, values, or occupational preference).
    2. Declarative knowledge (for example, know that).
    3. Procedural skills (for example, know how).

- Competency model is a framework for organising a collection of observable skills, behaviours, and attitudes that affect the quality of work people do. It describes what people need to know and be able to do in order to execute their responsibilities effectively.
- In terms of approach, there are various ways to drive organisational improvement, depending on organisational needs.
    1. A **core competency model** supports the development of those critical core competencies that are required by an organisation to achieve its defined strategy.
    2. A **technical/functional competency model** supports the development of technical, role-specific competencies that enable an organisation to execute more effectively.
    3. A **leadership competency model** supports the development of key leadership capabilities in order to build leadership impact within the organisation.
- Organisational change occurs when business strategies or major sections of an organisation is altered. It is defined as a change that has significant effects on the way work is performed in an organisation.
- 360-degree Feedback is a system or process in which employees receive confidential, anonymous feedback from the people who work around them. This typically includes the employee's manager, peers, and direct reports.

Questions for Discussion

1. What are the various components of competencies?
2. How is the iceberg model helpful in understanding hidden skills?
3. Discuss the 360-degree feedback and Delphi techniques in detail.
4. Describe the HR generic and Supervisory generic models of competency development.
5. Explain various causes of resistance for change along with the recommended actions for the same.

Project Questions

1. Compare and contrast the 360 degree feedback and Delphi technique of competency models. If your competency were required to be measured, which would you prefer to be gauged by?
2. How would freestanding organizations with limited resources select the core competencies that they wanted to use in the hiring of new staff?

...

Chapter **3**

Competency Categories

Contents ...

3.1   Introduction

3.2   Classification of Competencies

  3.2.1   Threshold and Differentiating Competencies

  3.2.2   Generic or Key Competencies

  3.2.3   Functional and Technical Competencies

  3.2.4   Leadership or Managerial Competencies

3.3   Steps in Developing Competency Model

  3.3.1   Determine the Objectives and Scope

  3.3.2   Clarifying Implementation Goals and Standards

  3.3.3   Create an Action Plan

  3.3.4   Identification of Individual Performance against Established Performance Criteria

  3.3.5   Define Performance Effectiveness Criteria

  3.3.6   Identify a Criterion Sample and Data Gathering

  3.3.7   Developing Interim Competency Model

  3.3.8   Validate Competency Model

  3.3.9   Finalise Competency Model

  •   Points to Remember

  •   Questions for Discussion

  •   Project Questions

Objectives ...

- To classify different categories of competencies based on their nature, importance and relevance.
- To understand the categorisation that provides easy understanding of competencies, and which are vital for job success.
- To study the steps involved in developing competency model

3.1 Introduction

There are certain capabilities, i.e. key competency people have and they need to develop it on a daily basis. A firm usually isolates several key skills or key competencies to look for in a candidate in an interview. One will be graded in terms of each competency based upon answers given to competency-based questions. Employers generally use some of the following as key competencies – teamwork, commitment towards work, career motivation, decision-making, communication, leadership, problem solving and so on.

Core competencies are those capabilities that are critical to a business achieving competitive advantage. The starting point for analysing core competencies is recognising that competition between businesses is as much a race for competence mastery as it is for market position and market power. Senior management cannot focus on all activities of a business and the competencies required to undertake them. Hence, the goal is for management to focus attention on competencies that really affect competitive advantage.

A competence which is central to the business's operations but which is not exceptional in some way should not be considered as a core competence, as it will not differentiate the business from any other similar businesses. For example, a process that uses common computer components and is staffed by people with only basic training cannot be regarded as a core competence. Such a process is highly unlikely to generate a differentiated advantage over rival businesses. However, it is possible to develop such a process into a core competence with suitable investment in equipment and training.

Globalisation and rapid technological change is a reality for companies today. It has changed the manner in which business has been routinely conducted and has brought into focus delivery of results in real time. Newer forms of organisational structures have emerged that are flatter with fewer hierarchical levels. Career paths are no longer linear and unbroken but are spiralling and lateral in nature. The traditional employment contract between employees and organisation has altered. While earlier, it was normal to assume a lifetime of security in exchange for doing a good job, now employees are increasingly looking for opportunities for professional development that will enhance their future employability.

All these changes have had implications for HR departments and performance appraisal in the new business context. Instead of evaluating primarily on the basis of quantitative results and on what is achieved, the focus is shifting to how it is achieved as an indication of an employee's ability to keep performing well in the future. It has made 'competencies' the new mantra for the HR departments aiming to effect change within organisations.

3.2 Classification of Competencies

3.2.1 Threshold and Differentiating Competencies

The characteristics required by a jobholder to perform a job effectively are called threshold competencies. These distinguish the people who can do the job from those who cannot. For the position of a typist it is necessary to have primary knowledge about typing, which is a threshold competency.

Basic competency required to do the job, which does not differentiate between high and low performance threshold competencies include basic knowledge, skills, traits, motives, self-image and social role, and are essential for performing a job. Without these, some areas of performance will be substandard. To move beyond minimal performance, additional competencies are required.

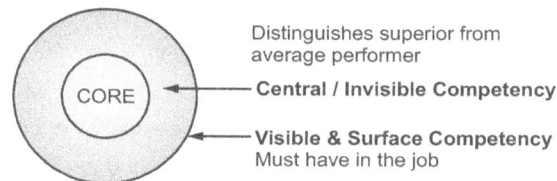

Fig. 3.1: Threshold vs. Differentiating Competencies

Threshold competency represents knowledge and skills related to a job whereas differentiating skills are those that distinguish a superior performer from an average performer. Attitude, values and self-image, achievement, orientation are examples of differentiating competencies.

Threshold competencies are like basic necessities to perform on a job but not sufficient to obtain superior performance and real success on the job.

3.2.2 Generic or Key Competencies

Generic competencies are considered essential for all employees regardless of their function or level. For example, communication, initiative, listening skills, etc. As the title suggests, generic competency means every employee should possess a certain competency that is common across the organisation or throughout the job like interpersonal skills.

Some skills are specific to the job of a person, like a HR person should know all HR related skills and knowledge about recruitment, training etc.

One can say general managerial skills are generic skills and certain technical and functional skills are key or specific skills.

3.2.3 Functional and Technical Competencies

Functional competencies are those that are required within specific functions, e.g. knowledge of products, labor laws, inventory distribution systems, local food safety and handling regulations. This type of competency relates to the functional capacity of work. It mainly deals with the technical aspect of the job. For example, market research, financial analysis, electrical engineering, etc.

"Functional competencies" are job-specific competencies that drive proven high-performance, quality results for a given position. They are often technical or operational in nature (e.g., "backing up an Oracle database" is a functional competency).

Competencies are used in human resources in a variety of ways. They describe the traits, skills and behaviours for a job role, they are used to establish performance and development criteria for performance management, they are used in the assessment of candidates for a position, and they are used in the assessment of people for leadership and new roles.

Technical competencies are specific competencies that are considered essential to perform a specific role in the organisation within a defined technical or functional area of work.

3.2.4 Leadership or Managerial Competencies

Leadership competencies are managerial and cognitive competencies. For example, analysis and problem solving, managing execution, adapt and learn etc. Leadership competencies are leadership skills and behaviours that contribute to superior performance. By using a competency-based approach to leadership, organisations can better identify and develop their next generation of leaders. Many essential leadership competencies and global competencies have been defined by researchers. However, future business trends and strategy should drive the development of new leadership competencies. While some leadership competencies are essential to all firms, an organisation should also define what leadership attributes are distinctive to the particular organisation to create competitive advantage.

Essential Leadership Competencies

A focus on leadership competencies and skill development promotes better leadership. However, skills needed for a particular position may change depending on the specific leadership level in the organisation. By using a competency approach, organisations can determine what positions at which levels require specific competencies. Researchers at the Center for Creative Leadership have identified some essential leadership competencies that are consistent among organisations. They divide the overall structure into competencies for leading the organisation, leading the self and leading others in the organisation. When selecting and developing leaders, HR professionals should consider the competencies that the individual possesses and compare those to the ones that need further development for success in a leadership role. By looking at his/her current competencies and comparing those to the skills necessary to fill a leadership position, organisations can make better-informed decisions in hiring, developing and promoting leaders.

1. **Leading the Organisation**

   - Managing change
   - Solving problems and making decisions
   - Managing politics and influencing others
   - Taking risks and innovating
   - Setting vision and strategy
   - Managing the work
   - Enhancing business skills and knowledge
   - Understanding and navigating the organisation

2. **Leading the self**

   - Demonstrating ethics and integrity
   - Displaying drive and purpose
   - Exhibiting leadership stature
   - Increasing your capacity to learn
   - Managing yourself
   - Increasing self-awareness
   - Developing adaptability

3. **Leading others**

   - Communicating effectively
   - Developing others
   - Valuing diversity and difference
   - Building and maintaining relationships
   - Managing effective teams and work groups

Managerial competencies are essential for managerial or supervisory responsibility (soft competency). This type of competency relates to the ability to manage the job and develop an interaction with other persons. For example, problem solving, leadership, communication, etc.

3.3 Steps in Developing Competency Model

Like any other development work, a foundation has to be laid in order to develop a model.

1. Determine the Objectives and Scope.

2. Clarifying Implementation Goals and Standards.

3. Create an Action Plan.

4. Identification of individual performance against established performance criteria.

5. Define Performance Effectiveness Criteria.

6. Identify a Criterion Sample and Data Gathering.

7. Developing Interim Competency Model.

8. Validate Competency Model.

9. Finalise Competency Model.

3.3.1 Determine the Objectives and Scope

Why are we doing it? What jobs, functions or business units will we target? What method will we use to develop the model? Who will carry out the work?

(a) It is important to identify the business need or needs that are to be addressed. This will help in ensuring continuous support for the project. Secondly, it will help the efforts of all participants to remain focused on the objective. It may also add to selection, training and development, performance appraisal, succession planning, compensation, etc. It should also address issues of attracting top talent, retaining key employees, ensuring that skills are available to meet the future challenges, aligning cross-organisational teams to get products to the market faster and aligning people's behaviour with organisational values and strategy.

(b) The objective and scope of the model needs to be focused on the targeted jobs, functions or business units, increase productivity or instill a specific company value. A competency model is most meaningful if it provides behavioural examples of identified competencies.

(c) While determining the objective and scope, it is essential to determine the method for developing the competency model. There can be two general approaches.

  • Starting from scratch

  • Starting with a validated competency model

If the objective is to develop a model for any job, function or role in the organisation, then starting from scratch is an appropriate approach. Here, data has to be internally collected from interviews with the incumbent and informed observers, focus groups and through on-the-job observations. This data must then be analysed to identify the competencies that are significant, to effective performance. Though this is time consuming, it focuses on role and company specific competencies.

Another approach is when organisations use a validated model as the starting point instead of extensive interviews and observations of incumbents on the job, thus saving time. However, such a generic model may not be role or company specific. It is best suited for managerial and leadership roles that cut across functions and positions.

(d) The project of developing a model should be assigned to a team of five to nine people depending upon the scope. The team should comprise of individuals who are responsible for implementing and using the model, key stakeholders, one or two individuals with experience and practice in competency model development and a visible sponsor who can act as its advocate within the organisation.

3.3.2 Clarifying Implementation Goals and Standards

What is the intended result of the project? How will we know when we have achieved it? To provide direction to the project the goal should be expressed in terms of performance or output. The goal should be specific, realistic, attainable, challenging, and consistent with the available resources. The organisation's measurable policies and procedures should have a deadline. To develop an excellent model, the implementation standards should address quality, quantity and timing. This should include a set of standards to identify what actions are to be taken to meet them.

3.3.3 Create an Action Plan

What are the tasks that are involved? Who is responsible for carrying them out? When must they be completed? What are the resources that are required? An action plan is essential to manage the workload, review, and monitor the progress of the project and communicate it to the team members. Another integral part is to identify the possible problems and be ready with a contingency plan to address those issues. An action plan should comprise of action steps broken into work that needs to be done, and deliverables into tasks and activities, accountabilities for carrying out each step, schedule specifying the set start, completion dates and various milestones and requirement of 'resources, including equipment, people, money, etc.

Certain problems are predictable and others are not. Advance planning for likely impediments will lessen their impact and minimise the impact of any unforeseen event. The problems that arise may be related to time and changed priorities, influence of stakeholders, power and political resources, resistance and skill. There is thus a need to review each step and plan as a whole, raising questions on what could go wrong where, and be ready with a contingency plan.

While developing a contingency plan, one must prioritise the listed potential problems that are most likely to arise in the implementation; determine the probability of each and the seriousness of its impact; assign accountability for these preventive measures; and draw up a list of contingency actions. This exercise would help in changing or modifying the course of action if needed, and provide people outside the project team with systematic information about the development process. Outgoing communication on the progress of the project is vital for its success. It helps reduce the likelihood of the project being stalled or derailed.

3.3.4 Identification of Individual Performance against Established Performance Criteria

What does successful performance on the job look like? Which job outputs or results will be examined? Against whose performance will the findings be tested? The identification of individuals at various performance levels is necessary when developing a model. First, there is a need to determine the successful performance related to job output or results and then to differentiate the behaviour of successful performers from that of those who are less effective. Once the performance criteria are agreed upon, an interviewing and observation pool has to be created in order to identify superior performers, mediocre performers and those who fall below expectations. Other alternative methods can be performance appraisals, ratings of effectiveness from direct reports and colleagues and inputs from a panel of judges. The quality of the performance criteria is very important because that would serve as the foundation for many steps and ultimately indicate the success of the model, ensuring that the people whose competencies have been identified have actually demonstrated these by successful performance.

It is essential to understand the business need that drives the project and identify the key success factors. The competency model should reflect the unique aspects of the position in a given organisation and not be developed in a vacuum. However, if for reasons beyond control, the objectives are changed during the development of the competency model it would mean compromising with the usefulness of the model itself. Therefore, the application of the model should not lose focus midstream.

3.3.5 Define Performance Effectiveness Criteria

This is one of the basic yet challenging phases in implementation of competency mapping project. Once, identification of job/ job families is done as the target of competency mapping, their performance effectiveness criteria should be defined. Unless, there is well-defined performance effectiveness criteria, identifying the competencies of performance becomes hazy. There is also a view that such setting up of performance effectiveness criteria is not a necessity since competencies that contribute for superior performance are only to be identified. This school of thought also does emphasise that defining such performance effectiveness criteria only results in duplication of effort since many of the data collection instruments used for identifying competencies do collect data similar to performance effectiveness criteria.

Therefore, there is a choice whether to define performance effectiveness criteria or skip it to address later during data collection phase. However, a brief description is given here. The following steps are indicative of actions to be taken as a part of setting up performance effectiveness criteria.

1. **Defining Performance Effectiveness Criteria Based on Secondary Data**

With a few exceptions, all organisations follow setting key result areas/performance targets as a part of performance management/appraisal. In these documents, what outcomes/deliverables are expected from each job is defined. Further, these documents also contain operational definition/meaning of superior performance, generally termed as outstanding or exemplary performance. Data of outstanding performance can be obtained with the help of these documents. It is an undeniable fact that it is difficult to gain such quantified performance targets in respect of many jobs especially in service and research-oriented organisations. However, even in such cases, some indicators of performance do exist. The performance targets, at outstanding level, can be used to define performance, effectiveness criteria for the jobs so identified for competency mapping.

2. **Collecting Primary Data on Performance Effectiveness Criteria**

Data obtained with the support of secondary sources can be complemented with primary data. The primary data can be obtained using the survey method. Employees performing the jobs, identified for competency mapping, their superiors, subordinates and customers can be surveyed by collecting their expectations of such jobs at outstanding level. All these data are consolidated for defining the performance effectiveness criteria. Alternatively, experts can be consulted to understand what call be the performance criteria far a particular job/job families.

3.3.6 Identify a Criterion Sample and Data Gathering

The objective of this phase is to collect all the relevant information for identifying the competencies of superior performance. At the end, this phase is expected to generate comprehensive data on technical, functional and behavioural competencies. Currently, a number of data collection methods are in circulation. Based on the requirement, an organisation can choose all the methods or some of them. Cost-effectiveness, user-friendliness, reliability and applicability are the issues that should be carefully evaluated while choosing a particular data collection method over others. Every data collection method has its own merits and advantages. However, various factors influence their actual utility.

Factors Influencing Data Collection Method

- **Types of Jobs:** Firstly, the appropriateness and effectiveness of data collection methods depends on the type of jobs to be studied. For example, critical incident, technique may be appropriate in case of administrative positions, because competencies in such positions are contextual sensitive. Similarly, card sort out method can be immensely useful for identifying competencies for a group of jobs/job families. For example, using this method, competency can be identified for people working in front office and sales in a hotel industry. Therefore, the first consideration should be the compatibility between the type of data collection method to be used and the nature of the job.

- **Operating Organisational Culture:** Prevailing culture of all organisations also play a vital role in choosing a data collection method. It has been the experience with some organisations that though the data collection method chosen was highly valuable but did not yield factual information due to non-support of organisational culture. For, example, interviews cannot obtain valuable information in case of some organisations where an element of distrust exists. On the other hand, interview may result in collecting some information that may work against the interest of identifying competencies. Therefore, data collection method must be adopted keeping in view the type of organisational culture.

- **Type of Organisation:** Some methods can be most suited to manufacturing organisations and some other for service-oriented organisations. Similarly, geographical spread of employees/operations and technology, demographics and educational profile of employees can have implications for the type of data collection methods to be employed.

- **Cost-effectiveness:** Cost in consonance with overall budget sanctions for implementation of competency management must be ensured. Some of the data collection methods can be cost-intensive since an organisation may have to hire the services of experts. For example, hiring case study writers can cost, whereas, the same can be dealt with by asking employees to write case studies themselves incorporating their critical experiences. However, the cost consideration should not override the concern for quality and reliability of information. Unilateral focus kind of consideration on the cost factor can defeat the basic purpose of competency mapping initiative.

- **Reliability:** This is the most important factor. Unless, the method employed is reliable, there is a chance of identifying incorrect indicators of competencies culminating in identifying wrong competencies. Data collection methods tend to be more reliable in some organisational contexts independent to their own reliability. Therefore, reliability must be given due importance in selection of the data collection method.

- **Resources:** Adequate infrastructure and availability of trained assessors is also a factor to be reckoned with while deciding on data collection method. It does not result in collecting valuable information if trained assessors are scarce, though the data collection method itself is valuable. Therefore, data collection method must be chosen according to the resource availability.

The most popular data collection methods are discussed in the following text in detail, keeping in view their significance in competency mapping. In practice, an organisation can choose few or more of these methods while considering the factors discussed above.

Classification of Data Collection Methods

Data collection methods used in competency identification can be classified into two types. Apart from these two methods, general sources such as studying generic competency models and competency card sort out methods are also used to gather the information.

1. Person-based Data Collection Methods

Data collection methods here focus on the characteristics of the person performing exemplarily on a job and amassing the data on desirable characteristics of a person to perform a job well. Behavioural Event Interviews (BEI), expert/focus group discussions, interviews, observations, critical incident technique, survey technique, 360-degree feedback, etc. are examples of person-based data collection methods. The objective of data collection here is to gather the information about the characteristics of job or job families.

2. Job-based Data Collection Methods

Focus here is on the job. The objective is to understand the kind of competencies required to perform the job well. Information collected in this type is used to complement the person-based information. Position description, job analysis reports, job descriptions, job specifications, performance plans, appraisals, training curriculum, daily logs, etc. are used to collect the job-related data.

Data collection methods play a central role in competency mapping as discussed above. Other methods of data collection are discussed as follows.

3.   Position-used data collection methods

The overriding concern of any data collection exercise is to collect the data in a meaningful manner so that it can be classified, analysed, interpreted and used purposefully. Therefore, data collection techniques should be used in a manner that avoid wastage of efforts and focus on the real issues. There is a misconception that all persons holding a particular job and job families will be interviewed, their job behaviour observed, and all such data collection methods will be used to gather information in order to identify the competencies. Such an exercise can become never-ending and can present a confused picture on competencies. Therefore, the first task in using position-based data collection method is to follow scientific criteria to collect the data. This criterion must lead to identify and select a sample that results in collecting valuable data for identification of competencies of superior performance,

3.3.7 Developing Interim Competency Model

This is the fourth point on development of the competency model. The information/data collected through interviews and focused group of jobholders as well as direct observation on jobs are analysed for identification of the most relevant competencies required for successful performance on job. The data so analysed will reveal the differences in the level of exceptional and standard performance reflected through the respective behaviours of the jobholders. The analysis will highlight the list of knowledge, skill and traits that are needed in performance of the respective job. This is the preliminary list of knowledge and skill and traits needed for the respective job, and this is known as the interim competency model.

The interim competency model will form the basis for any further additional collection of data. The model will be passed onto the stakeholders and the job holders for further improvements. This step involves reviewing the entire information/data available for arriving at a final decision as regards identifying the competencies for success on a particular job role or function.

Role of Data Analysis

At this stage of interim competency model, the interviewer takes the role of data analyst, He critically examines the entire data/information collected during the progress of interview and the subsequent observation study. The job to be carried out by the interviewer/analyst is divided into three phases or parts.

(i) Separate the comments given by the interviewees. The comments of the interviewees will throw light on the knowledge and skills that are required for performing the job in an excellent and standard manner.

(ii) Group the traits/characteristics, skill and knowledge into sets.

(iii) Give a particular name to each set.

The interviewer is advised to make a detailed cross-examination of the comments. As a result of the critical examination, one can see the emergence of themes and patterns.

Approaches for Developing Competency Model

Based on themes and patterns, the experienced expert consultant can quickly help develop the competency model. However, two approaches are useful for application in developing the competency model.

1. General Ideal Approach

The interviewer must be fully alert and listen to all that the interviewee states. In particular, note is to be made of the repetition of the respective skills and behaviour. This will show up the pattern of the behaviour skill and knowledge/traits needed repetitively irrespective of job in different situations, which will constitute the interviewers description of the way the existing situations are dealt with. This stage marks the beginning of broad themes in the process of intensive review of the information of data gathered.

Specific reference to the behaviour, skills, and knowledge in the context of traits can be grouped in one set. This is identifying a particular competency.

2. Blank Slate Approach

The interviewer is in a role of data analyst, takes notes and records any specific mention of particular knowledge, skill and traits used by the interviewee. Each time the interviewee quotes the particular knowledge and skill, the interviewer will show them under one group in his comments. In this way a number of groups can be formed. The groups can be given a name to distinguish one from the other in terms of competencies used in their respective conditions. Each group will reflect the competencies used in distinct conditions. Let us examine a few illustrative cases that were under study as part of the competency study in a brokerage company on the job of operations manager. This is an example of actual interview, comments of manager that indicate frequency of themes or patterns shown in the bracket and their respective competency is shown in parenthesis.

3.3.8 Validate Competency Model

The interim model is treated as work-in-progress, a hypothesis, and so the results are to be further tested and refined by a larger population of interviewers and observers from the focused group. Several pilot interviews and fine-tuning of the questions to be raised is desirable. This is a group activity. In the group process, an agreement on the questions is necessary, Personal biases and assumptions must be avoided at all cost and at all stages. These appear at the time of data collection and data analysis.

Data Collection

Data collection calls for an open mind, rethinking on the assumptions and developing new assumptions. In data collection, more number of people should be involved, but the same people should do the data analysis. At the end of data analysis, which will be done by teams of different persons, they will be required to support the analysis done by them.

In data collection, two methods are suggested: observe the job holders perform his job on typical days when he may look fresh and focused on the job; take a stock of the jobholder's behaviour through internal and external customers as well as the boss, direct reports and peers.

1. Schedule of Interviews

Schedule four interviews per day and allow half-an-hour break in between the interview to keep interviewers fresh and focused.

Validating and finalising the competency model is a big task. It is going to be based on extensive interviews and data analysis. The interim model of competencies is a hypothesis that is based on limited number of interviews, data gathering and analysis. The same is to be further tested and wherever necessary, refined. The whole process will involve a larger cross-section of the population and those who have a stake in the study.

The interim model needs to pass through the following.

(i) Validation Test: This means the competencies mentioned in the interim model are acceptable as valid and correct by jobholders. The result will be that the model will stand validated.

(ii) Competencies will be a Predictor of Highly Successful Performance: Once, the competencies are acceptable as valid, they are taken as a predictor of highly, successful performance on the job. This implies that the persons having these competencies will demonstrate these skills on the job.

Both validation test and predictor of highly successful performance involve the following activities.

(i) Testing of the model by focus group jobholders, groups and/or surveys.

(ii) Analysing the data of the focus groups and the data arising out of the survey and refining the model.

(iii) Validation of the model for co-relating the competencies with those of the excellent top performers.

(iv) Finalising the model.

The above four points are explained in detail below.

Testing the Model: At this stage, the interim competency model is to be tested for relevance as well as for exactitude/accuracy. A team consisting of a cross-section of jobholders and what we call the stakeholders (those who are interested in the designing of the model) will be involved in the process. The persons who are involved in developing the interim model will be excluded from this process.

The model will be circulated to a wider range of persons. The wider range of persons will examine/study the competencies to ensure that all the competencies are covered. The wider group of jobholders will include

(i) Cross-functional.

(ii) Functionalists from division locations. The idea being that competencies will be relevant and applicable to all places, divisions, taking into consideration the functional as well as regional differences. This process generates ownership to the work done and will be owned up by those functionalists who are likely to be affected by the model.

Data collection is done by two methods (a) focus groups and (b) surveys. These methods are time and cost-effective and will ensure views of the people who are holding certain positions and play specific roles and will ascertain that the skills, abilities etc. are essentially needed for successful performance of the job.

2. Focus Group Method

The focus group method will furnish full information about the interim model.

3. Survey Group

Survey method is another good method. The objective of the survey is to get the facts or new perspectives that may have been missed in the previous data gathering. In data collection, efforts are to include as many functionaries as possible. Views of those observers and the main stakeholders may open up new vistas/relevance of model to the respective model being performed. Here the aim is to involve people who know more about the facts. In this way, broader involvement of people will ensure their support to validate the model and acceptance for integration with the human resource system.

Survey is the preferred method for its wider coverage of study. The data emerging from the survey are dependable and accurate, demographically valid for different locations of the enterprise. Internal facilitators can help organise the survey with the help of external OD consultants.

In the case of focus group, the data is based on perception of many jobholders. Data information may contain divergent views of so many persons. Hence, the quality of data may suffer due to differing views. Organisation and conduct of focus group work is a little difficult because of the association of so many persons in the group. Thus, many preparations are needed to conduct focus group working.

In this context, to begin with, a training facilitator is needed. Jobholders or focus groups are needed to be communicated in advance to prepare for the discussion on competencies. A letter may be sent to the focus group that will contain the following questions.

(i)   The extent to which the competencies match with the most significant part of his job.

(ii)   The extent to which the behaviour in each group/category exactly define his job.

(iii)   You may like to add or delete the group/categories, but explain the reasons for your action.

(iv)   What suggestions you will like to make about the group/categories that make it relevant to your function? Explain the reasons.

(v)   Whether the title of group correctly represents the objective and behaviour.

(vi)   Any other observation you will like to make in order to make the model richer and more focused. The incumbent jobholder is also asked by letter to send any queries to satisfy himself about the model, and he should make it convenient to participate in the focus group data collection.

To summarise, the following points may be observed.

(i)   A group consisting of cross-functional groups of jobholders, and training facilitators take the lead in data collection. The jobholders are sent letters in advance to inform them of the data collection. Thus, they know in advance the objective of data collection and what is expected of them. This makes them ready to discuss the competencies. A letter in advance is to be addressed to the jobholders mentioning his designation, the time, date and venue of data collection. They are asked to review the interim model and see for themselves how far the competencies mentioned therein are applicable to their functions and duties.

(ii)   In survey, the interim competencies are used as checklist for comparison with what competencies actually exist used as per job holders, The respondents/job holders rate the competencies as relevant or irrelevant, and whether in frequent use or not.

(iii)   At this stage we need to get a confirmation that new data coming from the focused group or the survey are tallying with most of the job holders and informed observers, whether previous assumptions are accepted or not. Add any new item or eliminate the ones not important. Based on the new data arising out of the focus group data collection session, check whether previous assumptions on competencies are in conformity of the thinking of job holders as well as the bosses, peers or colleagues, etc., who are the informed observers in the process.

Analysis of survey data: The objective is to analyse and understand whether the interim competencies are seen as inevitable. The analysis may reveal significant differences between the views of different respondents. For instance, one group may consider risk taking as important for management positions and yet another group may not say so.

In analysing data, sophisticated statistical techniques like t-test, standard deviation and 1-way-ANOVA) are used for drawing conclusions. The mean, median, average score and frequency of responses are also helpful in arriving at some agreement amongst the groups. The sophisticated techniques however, are able to raise the confidence level to arrive at the final conclusion.

(iv) A draft model is developed based on the quality, information/data collected from the focus group and the survey data. The OD consultant involved in the exercise engages them in the refining exercise and in the process, some new data may have come to light or some data developed. A final model is prepared and sent across to the cross-section of people who are involved in the exercise. They will also give their comments. Finally, the key elements and the factors critical for success will be underlined.

In step two, the study has differentiated between the skills of top performers and average performers as also the critical competencies.

Since the interim model has been tested and refined, it is expected to have high face validity.

The client has to decide in which function he wants to use the model. In case it is to be used in the field of HRM for training and development function, the face validity of the model will be enough to ensure that the model includes the skills, traits and knowledge that are essentially needed for operation of jobs.

If the model is to be used in selection, compensation, appraisal, etc., then validating the model is imperative. However, the validating process is not absolutely essential, but necessary. Essentiality of the validating aspect is established more through creation of awareness or individual weakness, strengths and how the jobholders should perform/behave on the job. In the case of recruitment, the users in the company must fully understand how much the competency will predict about the success of a person performing the role in recruitment. Likewise, in performance appraisal and compensation one needs to understand how many times the successful managers use the identified competencies and what linkage it has in the productivity or rise in employee satisfaction or profit and sales. These competencies are used to arrive at the decision on compensation.

Validation study is a time consuming activity. It calls for specialised knowledge and skill in data analysis. The essential steps are

(i) Converting the group/list of competencies into 360-degree feedback questions.

(ii) Cross-section of job holders are classified into three groups

   (a) Those who far exceed the performing criteria

   (b) Those who meet the performing criteria

   (c) Those whose performance falls far below the performing criteria

(iii) Analysis of the data.

In conversion of competencies into 360-degree feedback questions, one has to pick up any observed specific behaviour that is representative of the job – from the competencies defined from refinement stage as well as from focus groups and interviews. The behavioural aspects may be so that they may be illustrative competencies,

Given below are the 360-degree set-tip questions, put in order to reveal the behaviour of jobholders. This shows capabilities, flexibility, adaptability and performance of a task.

The jobholder rearranges his own work schedule, to meet the business needs. The jobholder adapts to the work style of those whom he supports. The jobholder is proactive to help others keeping his own job. The jobholder will be able to meet the challenges resulting from the changing market.

The boss, direct reports of customers where necessary, and peers assess the significance of the capability. Assessment of the competencies of the jobholder based on the number of times the same was used against how many times they ought to use is done, based on rating skill.

In the case of big size enterprises, the 360-degree questionnaire is to select a group of 80-85 managers and in a small organisation, 10-15 managers. The performance of this select group of managers should be based on three criteria.

(i)   Above the laid down norms of the performance.

(ii)   At the laid down norms of performance.

(iii) Below the laid down norms of the performance.

The criterion is the one that was developed during the study of competencies, but the criteria must not be shared with the managers or anyone involved in the work. Each of these managers would be working with a minimum of three direct reporting subordinates and a minimum of three colleagues. The above points are essential to show availability of data based on which, analysis will be done and accurate results can be obtained using statistical methods.

Each of the managers is to be given a minimum of 10-15 questionnaires depending on the size of the managers. The managers will distribute the questionnaires to the direct reporters, the colleagues/peers and to the supervisors.

They are required to fill up the questionnaire. A consultant is helpful for maintaining anonymity and confidentiality.

The rating score is to be tabulated and analysed in respect of each individual manger. This is done to understand strength in relationship between capabilities, competencies and the aggregate assessed ratings of the distinct jobholders' performance. A significant linkage of competency with a high performing group is considered validity. Likewise, the competency rating score of high and low individuals is also examined.

In the case of low linkage between capabilities/competencies and the high performing group, the behavioural description is reviewed to get at the facts.

The performance criterion for selection of the groups of jobholders is most pertinent to get accurate results. The criteria are to be developed, to achieve accuracy and objectivity.

3.3.9 Finalise Competency Model

This is the final step. Analysis of the data from 360-degree feedback finalises the model by elimination of those items that have no correlation with effectiveness. At this stage, it is certain that the competencies along with the associated behaviour can be used as a tool-foundation for developing quality of decision-making in human resource development.

An illustrative validated competency model on management and leadership.

(i)   Envisioning the future.
   (a) Be a visionary and a strategist.
   (b) Be skilled to take strategic view of business objective in view of company's mission and vision.
(ii) Develop organisational values and encourage the organisational commitment to values in organisational functioning,
(iii) Be a strategic leader.
   (a) Be skilled to formulate plans/strategic thinking for the future.
   (b) Have leadership quality to articulate plans across the board.
   (c) Be a transformational leader.
(iv) Be focused on corporate governance and shareholders interest as well as ethics in business.
(v)   Be an effective team builder.
(vi) Influence others. Be participative in decision-making.
(vii) Be customer focused. Articulate concern for customer focus; meet customer needs.
(viii) Reward the best performers; institutionalise methods of rewards and compensation/incentives.
(ix) Be committed to total quality management system for spreading quality consciousness in all aspects of management functions.
(x)   Be skilled in calculating risk in the fast changing global market, in the interest of the growth of strategic business objective.
(xi) Be tactful and maintain good relations with government and other external agencies in the interest of promoting strategic organisational objectives.

Irrespective of where the competency model is to be used, its main objective is

(i)   To furnish a simple method for the users to define competency.
(ii) To recognise when it is to be used.
(iii) To evaluate how effectively it is done. (Lucia and Lepsinger, 1999)

Points to Remember

- **Threshold competencies** include basic knowledge, skills, traits, motives, self-image and social role, and are essential for performing a job.
- **Generic competency** means every employee should possess a certain competency that is common across the organisation or throughout the job like interpersonal skills.

- **Functional competencies** are those that are required within specific functions, e.g. knowledge of products, labor laws, inventory distribution systems, local food safety and handling regulations.
- **Technical competencies** are specific competencies that are considered essential to perform a specific role in the organisation within a defined technical or functional area of work.
- **Leadership competencies** are managerial and cognitive competencies. For example, analysis and problem solving, managing execution, adapt and learn etc.
- **Steps in Developing Competency Model**
    1. Determine the Objectives and Scope
    2. Clarifying Implementation Goals and Standards
    3. Create an Action Plan
    4. Identification of individual performance against established performance criteria
    5. Define Performance Effectiveness Criteria
    6. Identify a Criterion Sample and Data Gathering
    7. Developing Interim Competency Model
    8. Validate Competency Model
    9. Finalise Competency Model

Questions for Discussion

1. Classify different categories of competencies based on their nature, importance and relevance.
2. Define the following:
    - Threshold and Differentiating Competencies
    - Generic or Key Competencies
    - Functional and Technical Competencies
    - Leadership or Managerial Competencies
3. Discuss the steps involved in Developing Competency Model

Project Questions

1. Does competency management model contribute for professional growth of individuals? If yes, how and if no, why not?
2. Discuss why you might not wish to fly in an airplane if the pilot was selected on the basis of only core competencies?

...

Chapter **4**...

Career Development

Contents ...

4.1   Introduction

4.2   Career Planning

    4.2.1   Career Anchors

    4.2.2   Nature of Career Planning

    4.2.3   Objectives of Career Planning

    4.2.4   Process of Career Planning

    4.2.5   Advice on Career Planning

    4.2.6   Phases in the Career of an Employee

    4.2.7   Reasonability for Career Planning

4.3   Career Development

    4.3.1   Definitions of Career Development

    4.3.2   Theoretical Foundations of Career Development

    4.3.3   Objectives of Career Development

    4.3.4   Career Development Process

    4.3.5   Reasonability of Career Development

    4.3.6   Methods of Career Development Management

    4.3.7   Competency Approach to Development

    4.3.8   Career Paths

    4.3.9   Career Transition

- Points to Remember
- Questions for Discussion
- Project Questions

Objectives ...

- ➢ To understand the objectives of Career development
- ➢ To study the objectives and process of career planning
- ➢ To learn the reasonability of career planning and career development
- ➢ To be able to explain the methods of career development management
- ➢ To understand the terms like career paths and career transition

4.1 Introduction

Career Development is the lifelong process of managing learning, work, leisure, and transitions in order to move toward a personally determined and evolving preferred future.

In educational development, career development provides a person, often a student, and focus for selecting a carrier or subject to undertake in the future. Often educational institutions provide career counsellors to assist students with their educational development.

In organisational development (or OD), the study of **career development** looks at:

- How individuals manage their careers within and between organisations and,
- How organisations structure the career progress of their members, it can also be tied into succession planning within most of the organisations.

In personal development, career development is:

- *"... The total constellation of psychological, sociological, educational, physical, economic, and chance factors that combine to influence the nature and significance of work in the total lifespan of any given individual."*
- The evolution or development of a career - informed by:
  1. Experience within a specific field of interest (with career, job, or task specific skills as by-product).
  2. Success at each stage of development.
  3. Educational attainment commensurate with each incremental stage.
  4. Communications (the capacity to analytically reflect your suitability for a given job via cover letter, resume, and/or the interview process), and
  5. Understanding of career development as a navigable process. **(Angelo J. Rivera).**
- *"... The lifelong psychological and behavioral processes as well as contextual influences shaping one's career over the life span. As such, career development involves the person's creation of a career pattern, decision-making style, integration of life roles, values expression, and life-role self concepts."*

4.2 Career Planning

Everybody knows that leaving school does not mean the end of the learning. While our fathers may still believe in an 'iron rice bowl' or some sorts of lifetime job, we are well aware that in our rapidly changing society such things barely exist and what we learn at school is hardly sufficient to meet the demands in the job market. Once you start a working life, difficulties you meet on a daily basis will remind you of your own inadequacies and the need to explore new knowledge. Time moves on, so should you. Keep rethinking and revising your own career plan. The advice you get from this handbook can be applied repeatedly but with enhanced precision in different stages of your working life and will be a handy reference when you keep redefining your life goals through the years you live.

- *Career planning is a lifelong process to help you understand yourself and the external world, and to keep revising your personal goals accordingly. Some planning skills are involved. The model below explains how to manage the course of your career:*

- *Career planning is an ongoing process through which an individual sets career goals and identifies the means to achieve them. The process by which individuals plan their life's work is referred to as career planning.*

- *"Career planning is a process of systematically matching career goals and individual capabilities with opportunities for their fulfillment."*(**Schermerhorn**).

- *"Career Planning is a deliberate process of becoming aware of self, opportunities, constraints, choices, and consequences; identifying career-related goals; and "career pathing" or programming work, education, and related developmental experiences to provide the direction, timing, and sequence of steps to attain a specific career goal."* **(McMahon and Merman).**

4.2.1 Career Anchors

Career anchors denote the basic drives that create the urge to take up a certain type of a career. These drives are as follows:

1. **Managerial Competence:** Person having this drive seeks managerial positions that provide opportunities for higher responsibility, decision making, control and influence over others.

2. **Technical Competence:** People having this anchor seek to make career choices based on the technical or functional content of the work. It provides continuous learning and updating one's expertise in a technical or specialised area such as quality control, engineering, accounting, advertising, public relations etc.

3. **Security:** If one's career anchor is security than he is willing to do what is required to maintain job security (through compliance with organisational prescriptions), a decent income and a stable future.

4. **Creativity:** This drive provides entrepreneurial and innovative opportunities to the people. People are driven by an overwhelming desire to do something new that is totally of their own making.

5. **Autonomy:** These people seek a career that provides freedom of action and independence.

Career is viewed as a sequence of position occupied by a person during the course of his lifetime. Career may also be viewed as amalgam of changes in value, attitude and motivation that occur, as a person grows older. The implicit assumption is that an individual can make a difference in his destiny over time and can adjust in ways that would help him to enhance and optimise the potential for his own career development. Career planning is important because it would help the individual to explore, choose and strive to derive satisfaction with one's career object.

4.2.2 Nature of Career Planning

The following are the salient features of career planning:

1. **A Process:** Career planning is a process of developing human resources rather than an event.

2. **Upward movement:** It involve upward movement in the organisational hierarchy, or special assignments, project work which require abilities to handle recurring problems, human relations issues and so on.

3. **Mutuality of Interest:** The individual's interest is served as his needs and aspirations are met to a great extent and the organisation's interest is served as each of its human resources is provided an opportunity to develop and contribute to the organisational goals and objectives to the optimum of its ability and confidence.

4. **Dynamic:** Career planning is dynamic in nature due to an ever changing environment.

4.2.3 Objectives of Career Planning

Career Planning seeks to meet the following objectives:

1. To provide and maintain appropriate manpower resources in the organisation by offering careers, not jobs.

2. To provide environment for the effectiveness, efficiency and growth of its employees and motivating them to contribute effectively towards achieving the objectives of the organisation.

3. To map out careers of various categories of employees suitable to their ability, and their willingness to be trained and developed for higher positions.

4. To have a stable workforce by reducing absenteeism and employee turnover.

5. To cater to the immediate and future human resources need of the organisation on a timely basis.

6. To increase the utilisation of managerial reserves within organisation.

4.2.4 Process of Career Planning

Step 1 : Self-Assessment: The first and foremost step in career planning is to know and assess yourself. You need to collect information about yourself while deciding about a particular career option. You must analyse your interests, abilities, aptitudes, desired lifestyle, and personal traits and then study the relationship between the career opted for and self.

Step 2 : Goal Setting: Set your goals according to your academic qualification, work experience, priorities and expectations in life. Once your goal is identified, then you determine the feasible ways and objectives how to realise it.

Step 3 : Academic/Career Options: Narrow your general occupational direction to a particular one by an informatory decision making process. Analyse the career option by keeping in mind your present educational qualification and what more academic degrees you need to acquire for it.

Step 4 : Plan of Action: Recognise those industries and particular companies where you want to get into. Make the plan a detailed one so that you can determine for how many years you are going to work in a company in order to achieve maximum success, and then switch to another. Decide where you would like to see yourself after five years and in which position.

Step 5 : Catch Hold of Opportunities: Opportunity comes but once. So, whenever you get any opportunity to prove yourself and get into your desired career, try to convert it in every way for suiting your purpose. Remember, a successful professional is also quite opportunistic in his moves, examining every opening to turn to his favour.

4.2.5 Advice on Career Planning

1. Try not to waste much time and wait too long between career planning sessions.
2. Don't ever judge and analyse yourself, like your likes and dislikes, abilities, etc. by listening to what people around you say. Be your best judge.
3. Be open to constructive criticisms.
4. Career planning is a very important step that needs to be considered in totality. If need be, you should not be hesitant to take the help of professional guidance and find out the best career planning for yourself.

4.2.6 Phases in the Career of an Employee

Most working people go through career stages and it has been found that individual's needs and expectations change as the individual moves through these stages.

1. **Exploration Stage:** This is the stage where an individual builds expectations about his career. Some of them are realistic and some are not. But the fact is that these could be a result of the individual's ambitions.

2. **Establishment Stage:** This could be at the stage where the individual gets his first job, gets accepted by his peers, learns in this job, and also gains the first tangible evidence of success or failure. The establishment/advancement stage tends to occur between ages 25 and 44. In this stage, the individual has made his or her career choice and is concerned with achievement, performance, and advancement. This stage is marked by high employee productivity and career growth, as the individual is motivated to succeed in the organisation and in his or her chosen occupation. Opportunities for job challenge and use of special competencies are desired in this stage. The employee strives for creativity and innovation through new job assignments. Employees also need a certain degree of autonomy in this stage so that they can experience feelings of individual achievement and personal success.

3. **Mid-Career Stage:** The individual's performance levels either continue to improve, or levels, or even deteriorates.

4. **Late Career:** This is regarded as a pleasant phase, where one is allowed to relax and play the role of an elderly statesman in the organisation.

5. **Decline:** The stage, where the individual is heading towards retirement.

4.2.7 Reasonability for Career Planning

(A) For Individuals:

1. The process of career planning helps the individual to have the knowledge of various career opportunities, his priorities etc.

2. This knowledge helps him select the career that is suitable to his life styles, preferences, family environment, scope for self-development etc.

3. It helps the organisation identify internal employees who can be promoted.

4. Internal promotions, upgradation and transfers motivate the employees, boost up their morale and also result in increased job satisfaction.

5. Increased job satisfaction enhances employee commitment and creates a sense of belongingness and loyalty to the organisation.

6. Employee will await his turn of promotion rather than changing to another organisation. This will lower employee turnover.

7. It improves employee's performance on the job by taping their potential abilities and further employee turnover.

8. It satisfies employee esteem needs.

(B) For Organisations

A long-term focus of career planning and development will increase the effectiveness of human resource management. More specifically, the advantages of career planning and development for an organisation include:

(i) Efficient career planning and development ensures the availability of human resources with required skill, knowledge and talent.

(ii) The efficient policies and practices improve the organisation's ability to attract and retain highly skilled and talent employees.

(iii) The proper career planning ensures that the women and people belonging to backward communities get opportunities for growth and development.

(iv) The career plan continuously tries to satisfy the employee expectations and as such minimises employee frustration.

(v) By attracting and retaining the people from different cultures, enhances cultural diversity.

(vi) Protecting employees' interest results in promoting organisational goodwill.

4.3 Career Development

4.3.1 Definitions of Career Development

Career development is the series of activities or the on-going/lifelong process of developing one's career. It usually refers to managing one's career in an intra-organisational or inter-organisational scenario. It involves training on new skills, moving to higher job responsibilities, making a career change within the same organisation, moving to a different organisation or starting one's own business.

Career development is directly linked to the goals and objectives set by an individual. It starts with self-actualisation and self-assessment of one's interests and capabilities. The interests are then matched with the available options. The individual needs to train himself to acquire the skills needed for the option or career path chosen by him. Finally, after acquiring the desired competency, he has to perform to achieve the goals and targets set by him.

Career development is directly related to an individual's growth and satisfaction and hence should be managed by the individual and not left to the employer.

Career development involves managing your career either within or between organisations. It also includes learning new skills, and making improvements to help you in your career. Career development is an ongoing, lifelong process to help you learn and achieve more in your career.

- *"Career Development is an ongoing process that occurs over the life span, includes home, school and community experiences"*.   **(Pietrofesa and Splete)**

- *"Career Development is self-development over the life span through the intergration of the roles, settings and events of a person's life"*.   **(Gysbers and Moore)**

- *"Career Development is total constellation of economic, sociological, psychological, educational, physical and chance factorws that combine to sahpe one's career."*

(Reardon, Lenz, Sampson and Peterson; Sears)

4.3.2 Theoretical Foundations of Career Development

These include but are not limited to:

1. **Trait-Factor Theory:** The Trait-Factor theory of career development goes as far back as the early 1900's and is associated mostly strongly with vocational theorists **Frank Parsons** and **E. G. Williamson**. Some of the basic assumptions that underlie this theory are:

   - Every person has a unique pattern of traits made up of their interests, values, abilities and personality characteristics, these traits can be objectively identified and profiled to represent an individual's potential

   - Every occupation is made up of factors required for the successful performance of that occupation. These factors can be objectively identified and represented as an occupational profile

   - It is possible to identify a fit or match between individual traits and job factors using a straight forward problem-solving/decision making process.

   - The closer the match between personal traits and job factors, the greater the likelihood for successful job performance and satisfaction.

2. **Holland's Career Typology Theory**: An off-shoot of the trait-factor theory can be seen in the work of John Holland. Like the trait-factor approach, Holland's Career Typology focuses on individual characteristics and occupational task. Holland's theory expanded the concept of personality types and posited that:

   - Personalities fall into six broad categories: realistic, investigative, artistic, social, enterprising and conventional (often referred to as RIASEC).

- Since certain personalities are attracted to certain jobs, the work environments then reflect this personality and can be clustered into six similar populations (RIASEC).
- Although each individual is made up of all six types, one type is usually dominant. Most personalities tend to resemble up to three of the six personality factors.
- Personalities can be matched with similar combinations of work environments using a problem-solving approach.
- The closer the match of personality to job, the greater the satisfaction.

Holland's Career Typology takes a cognitive, problem solving approach to career planning and this model has been extremely influential in vocational counselling. It has been employed by popular assessment tools such as the Self-Directed Search, Vocational Preference Inventory and the Strong Interest Inventory. It has also resulted in practical resources like the Dictionary of Holland Occupational Codes which applies Holland's codes to major occupations.

3. **Super's Life-Span/ Life-Space Theory**: Donald Super believed that humans are anything but static and that personal change is continuous. Super's Life-Span/Life Space is a very comprehensive developmental model that attempts to account for the various important influences on a person as they experience different life roles and various life stages. Here are some of Super's main tenets:

- Every individual has potential. People have skills and talents that they develop through different life roles making them capable of a variety of tasks and numerous occupations.
- In making a vocational choice, an individual is expressing his or her understanding of self; his or her self-concept. People seek career satisfaction through work roles in which they can express themselves and implement and develop their self-concept. Self-knowledge is the key to career choice and job satisfaction.
- Career development is lifelong and occurs throughout five major life stages: Growth, Exploration, Establishment, Maintenance and Disengagement. Each stage has a unique set of career development tasks and accounts for the changes and decisions that people make from career entry to retirement.
- These five stages are not just chronological. People cycle through each of these stages when they go through career transitions.
- People play different roles throughout their lives including the role of "worker." Job satisfaction increases when a person's self-concept includes a view of the working-self as being integrated with their other life roles.

Super's theory has greatly influenced how we look at career practices. Understanding the ages and related stages of career development assists practitioners to identify where clients are in the career development continuum and suggest appropriate career related goals and activities. It also underscores the necessity to examine career development within the larger context of an individual's roles and life style and how to achieve a life/work balance.

4. **Krumboltz's Social Learning Theory of Career Choice**: John D. Krumboltz developed a theory of career decision making and development based on social learning. Career decisions are the product of an uncountable number of learning experiences made possible by encounters with the people, institutions and events in a person's particular environment. In other words, people choose their careers based on what they have learned. Krumboltz proposed that:

    •   The four main factors that influence career choice are genetic influences, environmental conditions and events, learning experiences and task approach skills (e.g., self-observation, goal setting and information seeking).

    •   The consequences of these factors and most particularly learning experiences lead people to develop beliefs about the nature of careers and their role in life (self-observational generalisations). These beliefs, whether realistic or not, influence career choices and work related behaviour.

    •   Learning experiences, especially observational learning stemming from significant role models (e.g., parents, teachers, heroes), have a powerful influence on career decisions, making some occupations more attractive than others.

    •   Positive modelling, reward and reinforcement will likely lead to the development of appropriate career planning skills and career behaviour.

Krumboltz saw his theory as:

1. a way of explaining the origin of career choice and

2. a guide to how career practitioners might tackle career related problems.

The practitioner starts with understanding how a client came to their career related view of themselves and the world and what is limiting or problematic about this view. Once this has been established, the practitioner and client identify what career relevant learning experiences, modelling or skill building will help them reframe their view. Using Krumboltz's approach a practitioner plays a major role in dealing with all career problems, not just occupational selection.

5. **Constructivist Theory/Models of Career Development**: Constructivist Theory of Career Development is related to existential theory and is more a philosophical framework within which career counselling can be done. Two thinkers associated with this approach are M. L. Savickas and Vance Peavy. Constructivist career development is based on the concepts of "constructivism" which include the following:

    •   There are no fixed meanings or realities in the world, there are multiple meanings and multiple realities. Individuals create or construct their own meaning/reality of the world through the experiences they have.

    •   People "construct" themselves and the world around them through the interpretations they make and the actions they take. These "constructs" or perceptions of events may be useful or may be misleading.

    •   Individuals differ from each other in their construction of events. Two people may participate in the same or similar event and have very different perceptions of the experience.

    •   People are self-organising and meaning-makers. Their lives are ever evolving stories that are under constant revision. An individual may choose to develop "new constructs" or write new "stories" in their life.

    •   To be an empowered or fulfilled person requires critical reflection of the assumptions that account for our daily decisions and actions.

    The constructivist career counselling approach is generally about life planning. The search for meaningful work is connected to constuctivism's emphasis on deriving meaning from personal experience. To have meaningful careers, individuals need to reflect on their life experiences and the resulting "constructs" they may hold about life/work/self. The client and practitioner work towards an awareness and openness of new constructs of one's life/work/self that can provide the basis for meaning. Interventions include working directly with the client's life experience and the use of meaning making processes such as narrative, metaphor, mapping and critical reflection.

4.3.3 Objectives of Career Development

Career development has become primary activity of organisations in order to create a pool of talented employees as well as enhance their career satisfaction. Along with this, it is also considered as an organised and planned process to improve the efficiency of organisation. In common terms, we may look upon it as an effort to strike a balance between organisational workforce requirements and individual career needs. Employees have their own personal desires and aspirations and need to effectively utilise their personal skills to attain their career goals and objectives. On the other hand, organisations have needs for staffing and meeting present and future human resource requirements. A career development system is a mechanism that takes both the parties in to consideration and helps them meet their requirements as well as objectives.

Objectives of career development systems involve:

- **Fostering Better Communication in Organisation:** The main objective of designing a career development system is to foster better communication within the organisation as a whole. It promotes communication at all levels of organisations for example manager and employee and managers and top management. Proper communication is the lifeblood of any organisation and helps in solving several big issues.

- **Assisting with Career Decisions:** A career development system provides employees as well as managers with helpful assistance with career decisions. They get an opportunity to assess their skills and competencies and know their goals and future aspirations. It helps them give a direction so that they can focus on achieving their long term career goals.

- **Better Use of Employee Skills:** A career development system helps organisation make better use of employee skills. Since managers know their skills and competencies and therefore, can put them at a job where they will be able to produce maximum output.

- **Setting Realistic Goals:** Setting realistic goals and expectations is another main objective of a career development system. It helps both employees and the organisation to understand what is feasible for them and how they can achieve their goals.

- **Creating a Pool of Talented Employees:** Creating a pool of talented employees is the main objective of organisations. After all, they need to meet their staffing needs in present and future and a career development system helps them fulfil their requirements.

- **Enhancing the Career Satisfaction:** Organisations especially design career development systems for enhancing the career satisfaction of their employees. Since they have to retain their valuable assets and prepare them for top notch positions in future, they need to understand their career requirements and expectations from their organisation.

- **Feedback:** Giving feedback on every step is also required within an organisation to measure the success rate of a specific policy implemented and initiatives taken by the organisation. In addition to this, it also helps managers to give feedback for employees' performance so that they can understand what is expected of them.

- **Other Objectives**
  - To help individuals cope with continued changes in the world of work.
  - To help individuals develop a realistic attitude toward the dignity of all work and workers.
  - To help individuals understand their unique abilities, interests, and aptitudes.
  - To help individuals develop a realistic understanding of themselves in regard to decision making and career alternatives.
  - To provide up-to-date occupational information and other labour market data.
  - To provide the opportunity for individuals to become acquainted with a wide range of occupational and educational opportunities.
  - To provide information about the work that will assist individuals in making long-range educational and career plans.
  - To assist individuals in making appropriate educational and occupational choices.
  - To provide appropriate follow up information.

A career development system can be very effective in creating a supportive culture in the organisation and help employees grow and utilise their skills to achieve their desires and aspirations related to their career. Both organisation and employees can meet their goals simultaneously.

4.3.4 Career Development Process

Career development aligns individual employee development with future organisational human resource needs to achieve an optimal match of individual and organisational needs and includes succession planning.

It can be understood from the following simple model of career development.

There are four steps to career development:

1. **Career need assessment:** Organisation provides ready access to an extensive list of competencies, functional opportunities, positions and other information that the employee can build into his/her development plan. Career needs to the employees can be judged by evaluating these competencies and potential using a variety of resources.

2. **Career vision:** Navigation of the career planning process may be linear, guided by a wizard, or non-linear, depending on the preference of individual employees. Career opportunities should be linked to the description, job specification and job design.

3. **Career action plan:** Career opportunities are aligned with appropriate development programmes to help employees integrate their developmental needs with orgnisational opportunities. An action plan is formulated to achieve the vision. The employee's supervisor may confidentially add his/her own comments to the employee's plan, including steps, timing and general comments.

4. **Monitoring career plan:** Senior management may be inturn, add confidential comments to an employee's plan and selectivity direct plans to a human resources contact for consideration for the talent management process to facilitate career movements of employees. It is important to monitor employee's progress towards the predetermined career goals.

4.3.5 Reasonability of Career Development

1. **Retain Top Talent:** Best-in-class organisations understand the need to retain their top talent. But the cost of retaining top talent can run in the hundreds of thousands of dollars to company expenses. Additional costs associated with retaining talent include the loss of company knowledge, disruption of customer service, and loss of morale and engagement in remaining employees. Providing career development opportunities ensures that valuable individuals are more likely to look within the organisation, rather than elsewhere, when they desire a job shift.

2. **Boost Engagement and Productivity:** Today's employees expect to find meaning and direction in their day-to-day work - not just jobs and tasks, but meaningful careers and career goals. Employees who have access to career development processes, resources, and tools feel much more engaged and supported by the organisation. In addition, employees who drive their own development are far more likely to be motivated and optimally productive on a consistent basis.

3. **Strengthen the Succession Pipeline:** The backbone of any effective succession planning process is a well-prepared talent pipeline that can be drawn from at any time. With an employee-driven career development initiative in place, your top talent gains the opportunity to apply for critical roles that may be vacant. Making such opportunities visible and available for all eligible employees ensures that the most qualified individuals enter those critical roles.

4. **Generate Knowledge Transfer and Retention:** With the current and impending retirement of millions of Baby Boomers and an aging workforce, it is crucial for organisations to retain the wealth of knowledge and experience of seasoned employees. Career development initiatives aimed at retaining experienced talent provide direct opportunities for knowledge sharing - enhancing and tapping into knowledge capital within an organisation, and ensuring that such valuable knowledge is not lost.

5. **Fill Internal Skill and Role Gaps:** Skill and competency gaps, particularly within critical high-level roles, are becoming more and more common as roles become more demanding and the demands of leadership grow increasingly complex. Creating a culture and process that facilitates internal mobility is one of the best ways to fill these gaps from within the organisation. An internal mobility framework enables qualified employees to find roles most suited to them, and enables the organisation to fill such roles without the extensive costs associated with hiring, training, and on boarding outside hires.

6. **Create Positive Employer Branding:** Organisations that achieve the most sustainable success are those that attract the best people to develop their strategies and achieve their goals. An effective career development initiative brands your organisation as one that truly cares about its employees, helping your organisation continuously attract the best people for the roles you need.

4.3.6 Methods of Career Development Management

Adopting a standard set of organisational career management practices helps support your business strategy in a consistent way. These methods, activities and opportunities sponsored by your company help employees meet or exceed job description requirements and achieve company goals. Typically, organisations manage this function by selecting specific top performers for development in strategic areas but also by providing development opportunities to the general population as well. Failing to define career management methods could lead to inconsistent application of HR policies. Resentment and inadvertent employee dissatisfaction might occur, leading to employee attrition.

(A) On-The-Job Experience

1. **Committees:** Committees are part of everyday activity in any organisation. They can also be effective learning tools, with the right focus. Committees made up of staff from different areas of your organisation will enhance learning by allowing members to see issues from different perspectives. Set aside part of the committee's work time to discuss issues or trends that may have impact on the organisation in the future.

2. **Conferences, Forums:** Employees can attend conferences that focus on topics of relevance to their position and the organisation. Upon their return, have the employee make a presentation to other staff as a way of enhancing the individual's learning experience and as a way of enhancing the organisation. (Some conferences and forums may be considered off-the-job learning.)

3. **Critical Incident Notes:** Day-to-day activities are always a source of learning opportunities. Select the best of these opportunities and write up critical incident notes for staff to learn from. Maybe a client complaint was handled effectively. Write

a brief summary of the incident and identify the employee's actions that led to a successful resolution. Share the notes with the employee involved and with others as appropriate. If the situation was not handled well, again write a brief description of the situation identifying areas for improvement. Discuss the critical incident notes with the employee and identify the areas for the employee to improve upon and how you will assist the employee in doing this.

4. **Field Trips:** If your organisation has staff at more than one site, provide employees with an opportunity to visit the other sites. This helps your employees gain a better understanding of the full range of programmes and clients that your organisation serves. Field trips to other organisations serving a similar clientele or with similar positions can also provide a valuable learning experience. Give staff going on field trips a list of questions to answer or a list of things to look for. Follow up the field trip by having staff explain what they have learned and how they can apply that learning to your organisation.

5. **Job Aids:** Tools can be given to employees to help them perform their jobs better. These tools include: manuals, checklists, phone lists, procedural guidelines, decision guidelines and so forth. Job aids are very useful for new employees, employees taking on new responsibilities and for activities that happen infrequently.

6. **Job Expanding:** Once an employee has mastered the requirements of his or her job and is performing satisfactorily, he or she may want greater challenges. Consider assigning new additional duties to the employee. Which duties to assign should be decided by the employee and his or her manager? Organisations with flat organisational structure are starting to give some managerial tasks to experienced staff as a way of keeping those staff challenged

7. **Job Shadowing:** If an employee wants to learn what someone else in your organisation does, the employee can follow that person and observe him or her at work. Usually the person doing the shadowing does not help with the work that is being done.

8. **Learning Alerts:** Newspaper articles, government announcements and reports can be used as learning alerts. Prepare a brief covering page, which could include a short summary and one or two key questions for your employees to consider. Then, circulate the item. Include the item on the agenda of your next staff meeting for a brief discussion.

9. **Orientation:** Introducing a new employee to the organisation, its mission, its activities and programmes, its clients and key staff are all part of orienting the new employee to the workplace. An orientation session is often the basis for an employee handbook. The handbook serves as a ready reference to the material

covered during the orientation session. The orientation of new employees can provide a great refresher or learning opportunity for their colleagues, who can be asked to present information or guide the newcomer.

10. **On-Boarding:** On Boarding includes orienting new staff to place, people and plans. It may include a preceptor or buddy system, series of meet and greets with key individuals, job shadowing, etc.

11. **Peer-Assisted Learning:** Two employees agree to help each other learn different tasks. Both employees should have an area of expertise that the co-worker can benefit from. The employees take turns helping their co-worker master the knowledge or skill that they have to share.

12. **"Stretch" Assignments:** These assignments give the employee an opportunity to stretch past his or her current abilities. For example, a stretch assignment could require an employee to chair a meeting (if the person has never done this before). To ensure that chairing the meeting is a good learning experience, the manager should take time after the meeting to discuss with the employee what went well and what could have been improved.

13. **Special Projects:** Give an employee an opportunity to work on a project that is normally outside his or her job duties. For example, someone who has expressed an interest in events planning could be given the opportunity to work as part of a special events team.

(B) Relationships and Feedback

1. **Coaching:** Coaching refers to a pre-arranged agreement between an experienced manager and his or her employee. The role of the coach is to demonstrate skills and to give the employee guidance, feedback, and reassurance while he or she practices the new skill.

2. **Mentoring:** Mentoring is similar to coaching. Mentoring occurs when a senior, experienced manager provides guidance and advice to a junior employee.

(C) Classroom Training

Courses, Seminars, Workshops: These are formal training opportunities that can be offered to employees either internally or externally. A trainer, facilitator and/or subject matter expert can be brought into your organisation to provide the training session or an employee can be sent to one of these learning opportunities during work time.

(D) Off-The-Job Learning

1. **Courses Offered by College/Universities:** At USF, employees can take advantage of the Employee Tuition Programme. Employees may attend these classes on their own time or your organisation may give them time off with pay to attend.

2. **Professional Associations:** Professional associations provide employees an opportunity to stay current in their chosen field.

3. **Reading Groups:** (Also called Learning Circles or Reading Circles) A group of staff meets to discuss books or articles relevant to the workplace/organisation. Meetings usually take place outside normal working hours, such as lunch time or right after work.

4. **Off-The-Job Learning, Self Study:** Self-paced independent reading, e-learning courses, and volunteer work all provide learning opportunities. The employee engages in the learning activity by choice and at his or her desired pace of learning.

4.3.7 Competency Approach to Development

New career realities require individuals to take responsibility for their personal career development. One effective way of supporting individuals in this challenge is through competencies. Organisations have been using competency models with the overall aim to improve individual performance. However, competencies as currently focus mainly on job-performance, neglecting other issues important for career development. This criticism was addressed by introducing the idea of career competencies as behavioural repertoires and knowledge that are instrumental in the delivery of desired career-related outcomes. A Career Competencies Indicator (CCI) was developed measuring seven areas of career competence:

1. Goal setting and career planning
2. Self-knowledge
3. Job-related performance effectiveness
4. Career-related skills
5. Knowledge of (office) politics
6. Networking and mentoring
7. Feedback seeking and self-presentation

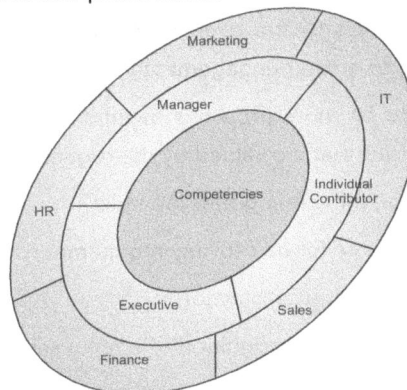

Fig. 4.1: Areas of Career Competency

Benefits of a Competency-Based System for Employers:

- Ensures that organisation-funded training and professional development activities are cost-effective, goal-oriented and productive.

- Enables employees to achieve a high level of competence in an efficient manner.

- Records the employee's acquisition of the skills, knowledge, safety and other procedures relating to each task.

- Reduces cost overruns caused by poor performance or miscommunication of job expectations.

- Improves communication between employee and management.

- Increases internal employee mobility, providing the organisation with greater ability scale and flex as needed.

- Establishes a framework for constructive feedback by management at scheduled training and performance appraisal intervals.

- Clarifies job standards for performance appraisals.

- Outlines employee development and promotional paths within the organisation.

Benefits of a Competency-Based System for Employees:

- Sets clear performance expectations for employees, enabling them to make better decisions and work more effectively.

- Gives employees insight into the overall strategy of their team, department, and organisation, leading to greater engagement and motivation.

- Enables employees to be more proactive beyond their individual roles, by learning additional competencies that are valued by the organisation.

- Provides clear direction for learning new job skills.

- Offers a reference resource for day-to-day requirements.

- Increases the potential for job satisfaction.

- Provides a mechanism for the recognition of employees' abilities.

- Ensures that individual professional development and training milestones are recorded and acknowledged by the organisation.

Career Competency	This competency is mainly about:
1. Build and maintain a positive self-concept.	• Self-understanding • Self-efficacy and self-belief • Positive attitudes
2. Interact positively and effectively with others.	• Communication • Working with others • Respecting diversity
3. Change and grow throughout life.	• Adaptability • Maintaining healthcare • Responsiveness to change
4. Participate in lifelong learning supportive of career goals.	• Transferable skills • Investing in learning to achieve goals • Commitment to lifelong learning
5. Locate and effectively use career information.	• Accessing reliable information • Learning from information • Interpreting labour market information
6. Understand the relationship between work, society and the economy.	• Work values • Benefits of work to individuals and communities • Impact of economic trends
7. Secure or create and maintain work.	• Effective job seeking • Creative ways of working • Using career guidance
8. Make career-enhancing decisions.	• Making choices • Decision-making • Problem solving
9. Maintain balanced life and work roles.	• Awareness of life and work roles • Life-work balance and well-being • Lifestyle
10. Understand the changing nature of life and work roles.	• Social and economic change • Equality and opportunity • Challenging stereotyping
11. Understand, engage in and manage the career-building process.	• Career planning • Career management • Risk and transition

4.3.8 Career Paths

Career paths employees need to know their strengths and weakness and they often discover those through company-sponsored assessments. Career paths represent employees movements through opportunities over time. Although most career paths are through of as leading upward, good opportunities also exist in cross-functional or horizontal directions.

Working with employees to develop career paths has aided employers in retaining key employees. For example, CDM, the operations, engineering, construction and consulting company based in Cambridge, Masschusetts, development career paths based on input collected from the key stakeholders including top leaders, scientists and engineers. These career paths reflected the most important competencies needed to accomplishment company objectives and proficiency levels and progression maps were established to guide how employees would move to job within and between career paths. The entire process was linked to the talent management and development programmes that existed in the company.

Career paths exist on an informal basis in almost all organisations. However, career paths are much more useful when formally designed and documented. Such formalisation results in specific descriptions of sequential work experiences, as well as how the difference sequences are related to one another. Career paths should:

- Represent real progression possibilities, whether lateral or upward, without implied "normal" rates of progress or forced specialisation in a technical area.
- Be tentative and responsive to changes in job content, work priorities, organisational patterns and management needs.
- Be flexible, taking into consideration the compensating qualities of a particular employee, managers, direct reports or others who influence the way that work is performed.
- Specify the skills, knowledge and other attributes required to perform effectively at each position along the paths and specify how they can be acquired. (If specifications are limited to educational credentials, age and experience, some capable performs may be excluded from career opportunities).

An innovative use of career paths called "skill supply chains" allows employees to move to other organisations as they succeed where they are. For example, in Philadelphia, more than 200 employers (fast-food restaurants, banks, supermarkets, retailers, hotels etc.) participate in a skill supply chain in the form of a "tiered employment" system aimed at underemployed entry-level workers. People enter the paths at tier 1 after receiving 4 weeks of customer service training and find themselves flipping burgers or cleaning hotel rooms. They have to be successful for 6 months, with counsellors checking attendance and performance. If they do well, they can apply for tier 2 positions either at their current employers or at another organisation in the system. After a year in tier 2, successful employees can apply for tier 3 jobs, which include entry-level store manager jobs. Viewing each job not as a dead end but as rung on a ladder makes people stay and perform well. This kind of career path system is based on the same drivers as those that operate in a private employer's career path system **(Raimy, 2002)**.

4.3.9 Career Transition

Careers work is no longer just about finding a quick fix solution to learners' needs at different career decision points. It is about equipping them for lifelong career well-being and happiness. Learners need to continue developing the career understanding and skills that will help them to succeed in learning and work throughout their lives.

Basically career transition is the process of finding and moving into a new career. There is no set period of time for career transition – and no limit to the number of times you might decide to change.

Interestingly, the transition period may start years before you consciously decide to make any change. It can include daydreaming about something you'd love to do, meeting people in careers that spark an interest, reading books or seeing films about things you enjoy, etc. as well as actually trying things on for size. And it may continue all the way up to and even after starting your new career, when insecurities and self-doubts can still creep in.

The emphasis on career-related change and adjustment over the course of careers is unprecedented. Issues of career resilience and multiple careers are paramount in current career theory (**Hall et al.,** 1986) and these issues highlight the importance of understanding how individuals manage increasingly frequent and stressful career transitions (**Hill, Miler** and **Lowther, 1981; Hymowitz, 1987**). In addition to rapid technological change, mergers and takeovers, downsizing and shifts in corporate strategic direction, there are value-laden questions related to work-nonwork balance, combing family responsibilities with career at different career/life stages and access of women and minorities not only to new occupations but also to upper levels without the organisation. These forces heighten concern about career stress of a transitional nature such as plateauing at mid-career or earlier, moving downward in the organisation, experiencing involuntary job loss, finding new careers at mid-life, adjusting to repeated changes in job responsibilities, interrupting or curtailing careers for family reasons, or early retirement **(London and Stumpf, 1986)**. As careers unfold over time, career transitions emerge as critical stress points that could have substantive impact on maintenance of employees emotional and physical well-being over time.

Therefore, a key departure point for integrating stress theory with careers is the concept of career transitions. A career transition has been defined as *"the period during which an individual is either changing roles (taking on a different objective role) or changing orientation to a role already held (altering a subjective state)"* **(Louis, 1980:330)**. Nicholson and West broader this definition to includes time when the job itself changes around an immobile incumbent, such as job redesign, change of boss, or co-workers. Thus, an inclusive definition of career transitions is consistent with the notion that a stressor situation can be externally or internally generated.

Points to Remember

- **Career planning** is a process of systematically matching career goals and individual capabilities with opportunities for their fulfillment.
- **Career anchors** denote the basic drives that create the urge to take up a certain type of a career. These drives are as follows:
  1. Managerial Competence
  2. Technical Competence
  3. Security
  4. Creativity
  5. Autonomy
- **Process of Career Planning**
  1. Self-Assessment
  2. Goal Setting
  3. Academic/Career Options
  4. Plan of Action
  5. Catch Hold of Opportunities
- **Phases in the Career of an Employee**
  1. Exploration Stage
  2. Establishment Stage
  3. Mid-Career Stage
  4. Late Career
- **Career development** is the series of activities or the on-going/lifelong process of developing one's career. It usually refers to managing one's career in an intra-organizational or inter-organizational scenario. It involves training on new skills, moving to higher job responsibilities, making a career change within the same organisation, moving to a different organisation or starting one's own business.
- **Career Development Process**
  1. Career need assessment
  2. Career vision
  3. Career action plan
  4. Monitoring career plan
- Career paths represent employee's movements through opportunities over time.

Questions for Discussion

1. Describe the objectives of Career Development.
2. Elaborate the objectives and process of career planning.
3. Discuss the reasonability of career planning and career development.
4. Explain the methods of career development management.
5. Define the terms career paths and career transition.

Project Questions

1. What career planning steps have you taken? What additional steps will you take based on educational progress or career progress?

2. Does career planning and development programme need to be integrated with organisational goals? Discuss with supporting factors.

■■■

Chapter 5

Innovative Employer Career Initiatives

Contents ...

5.1   Career Management

     5.1.1   Career Anchors

     5.1.2   Career Development Cycle

     5.1.3   Career Development Programme

     5.1.4   Organisation's Responsibility

     5.1.5   Different Methods used by the Employer to enhance Employee Career

     5.1.6   The Employee's Role

     5.1.7   The Employee's Role in Career Management

     5.1.8   Innovative Corporate Career Development Initiatives

     5.1.9   Special Issues in Career Development

5.2   Mentoring for Employee Development

     5.2.1   Mentoring Characteristics

     5.2.2   Mentoring Offers Several Benefits to the Protégé

     5.2.3   The Mentor also receives many Benefits from the Relationship

     5.2.4   Building One's Mentoring Skills

     5.2.5   Commitment-oriented Career Development Efforts

5.3   Managing the New Workforce: Different Career Development Needs

     •   Points to Remember

     •   Questions for Discussion

     •   Project Questions

Objectives ...

- ➢ To understand the objectives of career development
- ➢ To know the meaning of career management
- ➢ To study the role of the organisation in career management
- ➢ To learn the methods used by the employer to enhance employee career
- ➢ To be able to explain special issues in career development
- ➢ To understand the benefits of mentoring for employee development
- ➢ To elaborate various innovative employer career initiatives

5.1 Career Management

Career management is a process for enabling employees to better understand and develop their career skills and interests and to use these skills and interests most effectively, both within the company and after they leave the firm. Career development is a lifelong series of activities (such as workshops) that contribute to a person's career exploration, establishment, success, and fulfillment. Career planning is the deliberate process through which someone becomes aware of personal skills, interests, knowledge, motivations, and other characteristics, acquires information about opportunities and choices, identifies career-related goals, and establishes action plans to attain specific goals.

The employee's manager and employer should play roles in guiding and developing the employee's career. However, the employee must always accept full responsibility for his or her own career development and career success.

5.1.1 Career Anchors

Research has shown that certain attitudes are formed early in life to guide many people throughout their careers. These attitudinal syndromes serve to 'anchor' an individual to one or a few related types of career. An adequate knowledge of these anchors help in career planning and development. Five identified anchors are:

1. **Managerial Competence:** The fundamental characteristics of the individuals anchored by an overriding interest in management include a capacity to take responsibility, ability to influence and control others, and skills in problem solving. People who wish to be effective managers should possess competence in interpersonal, intergroup, emotional and analytical areas.

2. **Technical-functional Competence:** Their primary interest is in the performance of functional work. They want to be experts in their field.

3. **Security:** They are more attached to a specific organisation and area than to their work.

4. **Creativity:** They have an overriding interest in developing or creating something new. They become entrepreneurs and want to be identified with their product or service.

5. **Autonomy-independence:** They have an overriding interest in freedom and independence. They prefer their own working time. For example, consultants, freelance writers, etc. A HR manager must have knowledge of these basic drives and needs of employees while planning for their career development.

5.1.2 Career Development Cycle

A career involves various stages (Fig. 5.1). The stages are as follows.

Life Cycle of a Career

Exploratory Stage

↓

Establishment Stage

↓

Maintenance Stage

↓

Decision

Fig. 5.1: Career Development Cycle

1. **Exploratory Stage:** This is the stage when a fresh employee enters the organisation. The organisation should understand its responsibility towards the newcomer and try to prevent the reality shock by making the job challenging and interesting. Research has shown the more challenging the job is in the first year of service, the more effective and successful the employee will be 5 or 10 years later. Apart from initial training, the other approaches include 'sink or swim' meaning full-time training with no job responsibility, and work while training.

2. **Establishment Stage:** At this stage, the employee has chosen a specific direction. For a successful career development programme, an organisation is required to feed back the progress information to the employee. For example, first performance appraisal, first promotion, first completed project assignment, first foreign trip are all extremely important occasions in a young person's career.

3. **Maintenance Stage:** This is the stage when an employee attempts to retain what he or she has established in the career. In today's competitive and dynamic business environment, this requires continued learning and updating in order to maintain their continuity with the organisation. This is the stage where an employee faces mid-career crisis. In some cases, people try to switch over to an entirely different job. For example, an employee leaves a factory job for a teaching profession.

4. **Decline:** This is the stage of retirement, depressing but inevitable. The organisation should ensure a smooth retirement event.

5.1.3 Career Development Programme

A well-designed career development programme has the following three stages.

1. **Career Need Assessment:** This refers to assisting employers in assessing their own personal career needs. Often employees are uncertain as to which type of work will suit them. A HR manager should help them in this decision-making process. A number of evaluation instruments are available that help a person in determining his or her main interests and basic aptitudes. For example, Strong's Vocational Interest Blank. This helps individuals to do their own career planning.

2. **Career Opportunities:** As employees have definite career needs, it is obligatory on the part of an organisation to chart out specific career paths through the organisation. Employees want to know what types of job are there at present and what will be available in the near future; what type of duties are to be performed; whether any training and development is required or not; and what jobs lead to other jobs in the organisation.

3. **Need-opportunity Alignment:** After the employees have assessed their career needs and have become aware of organisational career opportunities, rest is the alignment of need and opportunities. Now, a HR manager should select suitable development techniques, for example, special assignment, planned position rotation, coaching, mentoring, etc. Few developmental techniques have been discussed earlier in this chapter.

5.1.4 Organisation's Responsibility

An organisation and its managers can play a very influential role in a person's career development. A manager should provide developmental assignments to an employee and provide him constructive and timely performance feedback. The employer can provide career-oriented training and development opportunities, offer career management programmes and establish career-oriented performance appraisal and job-posting policies. The essence of a progressive career development programme is built on providing support for employees to continually add to their skills, abilities and knowledge and for this the set by logical sequence of steps includes

1. Clearly communicating the organisation's goals and future strategies to its people so that they know the target set by the organisation and how they can themselves develop to achieve this.
2. Creating growth opportunities and provide employees new, interesting and challenging tasks.
3. Offering financial assistance in the form of tuition reimbursement to ensure they retain current knowledge.
4. Providing paid time off from work, for off-the-job training and development.

For instance, a college, university or UGC supports a teacher/lecturer in his career development such as providing him paid study leave to go for a higher degree like Ph.D., financial support for research projects, payment for attending conferences and seminars nationally as well as internationally, refresher courses, etc.

In addition to the above-mentioned steps, an employer can take other steps like the following.

1. **Realistic Job Previews:** Providing realistic job previews before actually hiring a person is very important. Realistic job previews can help prospective employees more accurately gauge whether the job is indeed for them and particularly whether a job's demands are a good fit with a candidate's skills and interests. This is especially important for a fresh candidate whose confidence is yet to build up. By providing interesting and challenging jobs to a fresh candidate, an employer can prevent reality shock. Reality shock is a phenomenon that occurs when the new employee's high job expectations meet/confront with the reality of a boring, uninteresting and unchallenging job.

2. **Career-oriented Appraisals:** In this the supervisor or manager is so trained that not only he appraises the employee's performance but also aligns that performance with the feasible career path and finds out where training and development is required.

3. **Planned Job Rotation:** This refers to well-planned movement of an employee from one position to another in order to enhance his or her role with the organisation.

4. **Mentoring:** A mentor is an older and respected manager or professional who counsels and listens for feelings as well as facts and stimulates people through ideas and information. Mentoring is a developmentally oriented relationship between senior and junior colleagues or peers that involves advising, role modeling, sharing contacts and giving general support. Mentoring can be voluntary and informal or involuntary and formal. Informal mentoring is generally more effective than mentoring done solely as a formal responsibility.

5. **Job-posting:** This refers to the announcement of job openings in the company bulletin board, or in a company's newsletter. Job-posting system has the advantage of reinforcing the notion that the organisation promotes from within.

6. **Coaching:** It refers to meetings and discussions between a manager and his or her employee regarding the individual's career development. Coaching involves the setting of a conducive environment, actively listen to employee, ask questions and provide useful feedback.

5.1.5 Different Methods used by the Employer to enhance Employee Career

1. **Training:** A well-designed training program that maximises learning before, during and after instruction, translates into positive, lasting changes on the job.

   Effective programs can include orientation, on-the-job training and classroom instruction.

   Internet-based learning is an increasingly attractive option that allows employees to learn at their own pace and on their own schedule (on weekends or evenings) with access to the material at any time.

2. **Self-directed Learning:** This approach puts individual employees in control of their own learning, allowing for personal differences in learning styles and encouraging ownership of the learning process.

   When using this approach, many employers work with employees to develop a learning contract or personal development plan. The contract or plan is signed by both parties and outlines clear learning goals.

3. **Coaching and Mentoring:** Demonstrated benefits of these approaches include improved quality and quantity of work, transfer of learning and, for employees, improved communication and problem-solving skills.

   Effective coaching and mentoring programs depend on the skills and personality of the mentor or coach, adequate time for coaching and mentoring sessions, and established timelines and goals.

4. **Employee Promotion:** Promoting someone to a position of greater responsibility is a traditional way of rewarding good performance, developing employee skills and retaining valued employees.

   Effective promotion involves careful consideration of many details, including identifying gaps in skills and experience and providing support through training, coaching or mentoring.

5. **Job enrichment:** Job enrichment increases the employee's authority or responsibility within their current position. Examples include committee work, special assignments or serving on cross-functional teams.

   This approach increases interest and motivation by allowing employees to try new skills, build new relationships and explore new areas of specialisation.

6. **Job Rotation and Cross Training:** Job rotation moves an employee through one or more different positions. The rotation can last several days, several months or even a year or two. Cross training is a specific type of job rotation where an employee learns the skills of a different position.

    These approaches can effectively add diversity and interest, prepare individuals for promotion, rejuvenate work units and improve communication.

7. **Lateral Moves:** In a lateral move, an employee moves to a different position with similar status, pay and responsibility. A lateral move may offer new challenges or encourage the development of different skills for an employee who may not necessarily want increased responsibility.

    This approach increases flexibility and communication among work units, and in small businesses with few opportunities for advancement, helps to retain valuable employees who might otherwise leave.

8. **Job Aids:** Job aids include checklists, tip sheets, wallet cards, posters, pictures, code lists, flow charts and diagrams—anything that offers on-the-spot practical help or reminders. Job aids can reduce the amount of information employees need to recall by providing easily accessible facts.

    Well-designed job aids are concise, written in plain language and make good use of white space and graphics for easy interpretation.

5.1.6 The Employee's Role

For the employee, career planning means matching individual strengths and weaknesses with occupational opportunities and threats. The person wants to pursue occupations, jobs, and a career that capitalises on his or her interests, aptitudes, values and skills. He or she also wants to choose occupations, jobs, and a career that makes sense in terms of projected future demand for various types of occupations.

1. **Skills and Aptitudes:** The process logically starts with identifying one's occupational strengths, weaknesses, preferences, aptitudes, and skills. Career counseling expert, John Holland, says that personality (including values, motives, and needs) is one career choice determinant. For example, a person with a strong social orientation might be attracted to careers that entail interpersonal rather than intellectual or physical activities and to occupations such as social work. Based on research with his Vocational Preference Test (VPT), Holland found six basic personality types or orientations. Individuals can use his Self Directed Search (SDS) test (available at www.self-directed-search.com) to assess their occupational orientations and preferred occupations.

The SDS has an excellent reputation, but the career seeker needs to be somewhat wary of some of the other online career assessment sites. One study of 24 no-cost online career assessment websites concluded that they were easy to use, but suffered from insufficient validation and confidentiality. However, a number of online career assessment instruments such as Career Key (www.careeerkey.org) do reportedly provide validated and useful information.

2. **Identify High-Potential Occupations:** Learning about yourself is only half the job of choosing an occupation. You also have to identify those occupations that are right (given your occupational orientations, skills, career anchors and occupational preferences) as well as those that will be in high demand in the years to come.

Sometimes, there is no good substitute for actually trying a variety of jobs. Another useful way to learn, compare and contrast occupations is through the Internet. For example, the US Department of Labor's online (www.bis.gov/oca) Occupational Outlook Handbook (updated each year) provides detailed descriptions and information on hundreds of occupations.

Should a person change jobs? An employee unhappy with his or her job can do several things short of changing occupations. First, if you are satisfied with your occupation and where you work but not with your job at present, reconfigure your job. For example, consider alternative work arrangements such as part-time work, flexible hours, or telecommuting; delegate or eliminate the job functions that you least prefer; and seek out a "stretch assignment" that will let you work on something that you find challenging. Second, enhance your networks. For instance, discuss your career goals with role models or become a board member for a nonprofit organisation so you can interact with new people.

3. **Mentoring:** Having a mentor – a senior person who is a sounding board for career questions and concerns, and who provides career related guidance and support – could significantly enhance career satisfaction and success. Suggestions for finding and using a mentor include

- Choose an appropriate potential mentor. The mentor should be able to remain objective to offer good career advice.

- Make it easier for a potential mentor to agree to your request by clarifying what you expect in terms of time and advice.

- Have an agenda. Bring an agenda to your first mentoring meeting that lays out key issues and topics for discussion.

- Respect the mentor's time. Be selective about the work-related issues that you bring to the table.

- Mandatory mentoring is okay. Studies suggest that mandatory participation is no less effective than voluntary participation in a mentoring program.
- Match mentors. Both the mentor and a protégé should have some influence on whom the company matches them to.
- Provide training. Finally, provide participants with training aimed at enabling them to get the most out of the mentoring relationship.

Many employers, like Charles Schwab and Bank of America, offer formal mentoring programs. The accounting firm KPMG made an online mentoring program part of its "employer of choice" initiative. This program also includes shared time off, flexible work schedules, and community volunteer opportunities with pay and benefits. Dow Chemical Co. has a web-based mentor technology similar to a Google search. It enables Dow employees who are seeking mentors to screen lists of potential Dow mentors online.

5.1.7 The Employee's Role in Career Management

The employer's career development tasks depend partly on how long the employee has been with the firm. Before hiring, realistic job interviews can help prospective employees more accurately gauge whether the job is a good fit with a candidate's skills and interests.

Especially for recent college graduates, the first job can be crucial for building confidence and a more realistic picture of what he or she can and cannot do. Providing challenging first jobs (rather than relegating new employees to "jobs where they can't do any harm") and having an experienced mentor who can help the person learn the ropes are important. Some refer to this as preventing reality shock, a phenomenon that occurs when a new employee's high expectations and enthusiasm confront the reality of a boring, unchallenging job.

After the person has been on the job for a while, new career management roles arise. Career-oriented appraisals in which the manager is trained not just to appraise the employee but also to match the person's strengths and weaknesses with a feasible career path and required development work is one important step. Similarly, providing periodic job rotation can help the person develop a more realistic picture of what he or she is (and is not) good at, and thus the sort of future career moves that might be best. Some innovative career development activities include

1. Provide each employee with an individual career development budget. He or she can use this budget for learning about career options and personal development.
2. Offer online career centres. These might include career development materials, career workshops, and individual career coaches for career guidance.
3. Encourage role reversal. Have employees temporarily work in different positions in order to develop a better appreciation of their occupational strengths and weaknesses.

A list of HR activities that can influence and support employee career planning and development.

- Job postings.
- Formal education/tuition reimbursement.
- Performance appraisal for career planning.
- Counselling by manager.
- Lateral moves/job rotations.
- Counselling by HR.
- Pre-retirement programs.
- Succession planning.
- Dual ladder programs (options for non-managers to move up).
- Career booklets/pamphlets.
- Written individual career plans.
- Career workshops.
- Assessment centre.
- Peer appraisal.
- Upward appraisal.
- Appraisal committees.
- Training programs for managers.
- Orientation/inclusion programs.
- Diversity management.
- Expatriation/repartition.

5.1.8 Innovative Corporate Career Development Initiatives

Employer's corporate career development initiatives may also include innovative programs like these.

1. Provide each employee with an individual career development budget. He or she can use this budget for learning about career options and personal development.

2. Offer on-site or online career centres. These might include an on- or offline library of career development materials, career workshops, and individual career coaches for career guidance,

3. Encourage role reversal. Have employees temporarily work in different positions to develop a better appreciation of their occupational strengths and weaknesses.

4. Provide career coaches. The coaches help individual employees identify their development needs and obtain the training, professional development, and networking opportunities that they need.

5. Provide career-planning workshops. A career-planning workshop is a planned learning event in which participants are expected to be actively involved, completing career planning exercises and inventories and participating in career skills practice sessions.

6. Computerised on- and offline programs are available for improving the organisational career-planning process, For example, employees can use Self Directed Search (www.self-directed-search.com) to identify career preferences.

5.1.9 Special Issues in Career Development

There are many special issues with respect to career development. Careers are not always made up of progressive steps up the hierarchical ladder. People retire, organisations downsize and careers reach an apex and plateau through no fault of the employee, and women and minorities still have difficulties in reaching top positions. These issues are discussed in the following sections.

1. Gender Issues in Career Development

Women and men face different challenges as they advance through their careers. In one study, promoted women had to receive higher performance ratings than promoted men to be promoted, "suggesting that women were held to stricter standards for promotion." Women also report greater barriers (such as being excluded from informal networks) than do men, and more difficulty getting developmental assignments and geographic mobility opportunities. Because developmental experiences like these are so important, organisations that are interested in helping female managers advance should focus on breaking down barriers that interfere with women's access to developmental experiences.

Minority Women: In these matters, minority women seem particularly at risk. Women of color hold only a small percentage of professional and managerial private sector positions.

Adding to the problem is the fact that some corporate career development programs may be inconsistent with the needs of minority (and non-minority) women. For example, such programs may assume that career paths are continuous; yet the need to stop working for a time due to family issues punctuates the career paths of many women (and, often men). One study concluded that fast-track development programs, individual career counselling, and career-planning workshops were less available to women than to men. Many refer to this combination of subtle and not-so-subtle barriers to women's career progress as the glass ceiling.

2. Managing Employees' Promotions and Transfers

Promotions are, of course, one of the more significant HR decisions to result from the performance appraisal. In developing promotion policies, employers need to address several issues.

One issue concerns seniority versus competence. Competence is normally the basis for promotions, although in many organisations civil service or union requirements and similar constraints still give an edge to seniority.

Furthermore, if competence is to be the basis for promotion, how should we measure it? Defining past performance is usually straightforward. Managers use performance appraisals for this. However, sizing up how even a high-performing employee will do in a new job is not so easy. Innumerable great salespeople turn out to be awful managers, for instance. Many employers therefore use formal selection devices like tests and assessment centres to supplement the performance appraisals.

With more companies downsizing and flattening their organizations, promotions today often mean lateral moves or transfers. In such situations, the promotional aspect is not so much a higher-level job or more pay, but the opportunity to assume new, same level responsibilities (such as a salesperson moving into HR) or increased decision-making responsibilities within the same job.

A transfer is a move from one job to another, usually with no salary or grade change. Employees may seek transfers not just for advancement but also for non-career reasons, such as better hours, location of work, and so on.

3. Retirement

For most employees, years of appraisals and career development end with retirement. Retirement planning is now a significant issue for employers. In the United States, the number of 25 to 34-year olds is growing relatively slowly, and the number of 35 to 44-year olds is declining. With many older employees moving into the traditional 60 plus retirement age, employers will face a labor shortage. Many have wisely chosen to fill their staffing needs in part with current or soon-to-be retirees.

Therefore, "retirement planning" is no longer just for helping current employees slip into retirement. It should also enable the employer to retain, in some capacity, the skills and brainpower of those who would normally leave the firm. Fortuitously, 78% of employees in one survey said they expect to continue working in some capacity after normal retirement age. 64% said they want to do so part time. Only about a third said they plan to continue work for financial reasons, about 43% said they just wanted to remain active.

Not surprisingly, studies show that employees who are more committed and loyal to the employer are more likely to stay beyond their normal retirement age. Beyond that, specific suggestions include

- **Create a Culture that Honors Experience:** For example, the CVS pharmacy chain works through the National Council on Aging, city agencies and community organisations to find such employees. They have also made it clear to retirees with their policies that they welcome older workers. As one dedicated older worker said, "I am too young to retire. CVS is willing to hire older people. They do not look at your age but your experience."

- **Modify Selection Procedures:** For example, one British bank stopped using psychometric tests, replacing them with role-playing exercises to gauge how candidates deal with customers.

- **Offer Flexible Work:** Companies need to design jobs such that the staying is more attractive than leaving. One of the simplest ways to do this is through flexible work, in terms of hours and telecommuting.

- **Phased Retirement:** Phased retirement programs combine reduced work hours, job change, and reduced responsibilities, to extend the employee participation in the company.

Employers should conduct the necessary numerical analysis for dealing with the prospect of retirements. This assessment should include such things as a demographic analysis of the company's employees and a determination of the average retirement age for the company's employees. The employer can then determine the extent of the "'retirement problem" and take fact-based steps to address it.

5.2 Mentoring for Employee Development

To provide employees with development opportunities, an increasing number of organisations are turning to mentoring programs. Some companies incorporate mentoring as a stand-alone tool; others use it to supplement formal training. Regardless, these programs can be an effective way to improve employee performance.

Mentoring centres on a relationship between an employee who has potential (the protégé) and a colleague with expertise (the mentor). The protégé seeks the support and training of the mentor in order to learn and develop specific skills. The mentor, passing on knowledge and insight and offering direction, serves as a subject matter expert and a role model for the protégé. Mentoring relationships can range anywhere from a three-month engagement to an entire professional career. Protégés may have several mentors over their professional life or one mentor to carry them throughout their career. The mentor often works within the organisation, although he or she could be a professional contact outside of the organisation.

Mentoring is a formal or informal relationship established between an experienced, knowledgeable employee and an inexperienced or new employee. The purpose of the mentoring relationship is to help the new employee quickly absorb the organisation's cultural and social norms. Mentoring also assists employees, new to a specific job or area of responsibility to learn what they need to know to succeed in their job and role.

Mentoring can involve a formal exchange of knowledge and information and can be evaluative in nature to assess the assimilation of the new employee in his or her new role. Mentoring is provided to the new employee and should have different content and goals.

The best mentoring relationships involve the exchange of a particular body of knowledge that helps the new employee quickly come up to speed as a contributor within the organisation. Mentoring helps the employee navigate the learning curve inherent in any new role and relationship.

Many organisations assign a mentor as part of their formal employee on-boarding process. Other mentoring relationships develop spontaneously and over time. All mentoring relationships are encouraged as research indicates that employees who experience mentoring remain, learn more quickly, and assimilate into the company culture more effectively.

A mentoring relationship frequently occurs between an employee and their immediate supervisor; in fact, this was the normal mentoring relationship in the past. These mentoring relationships are still encouraged but it is recommended that employees and organisations pursue additional mentoring relationships. A mentoring relationship with a supervisor never loses the evaluation aspects necessary for the employee to succeed within the organisation.

5.2.1 Mentoring Characteristics

- Take place outside of a line manager-employee relationship, at the mutual consent of a mentor and the person being mentored.

- Is career-focused or focuses on professional development that may be outside a protégé's area of work.

- Relationship is personal, a mentor provides both professional and personal support.

- Relationship is initiated by a mentor or created through a match initiated by the organisation.

- Relationship crosses job boundaries.

- Relationship may last for a specific period of time (nine months to a year) in a formal program, at which point the pair may continue in an informal mentoring relationship.

5.2.2 Mentoring Offers Several Benefits to the Protégé

1. It shortens the learning curve for professional growth.

2. It helps the protégé develop new professional relationships within the organisation.

3. It provides a sounding board and safe place to share ideas and thoughts.

4. It challenges the protégé to go further, take risks, and set new goals.

5. It offers a rich and customised learning environment.

6. It enhances the protégé's network of professional role models.

7. It improves the protégé's self-awareness.

8. It demonstrates that the organisation is committed to the protégé's professional growth and development.

5.2.3 The Mentor also receives many Benefits from the Relationship

1. Mentoring allows the mentor to share knowledge and experience.

2. It helps the mentor learn from new ideas and different viewpoints.

3. It gives the mentor satisfaction knowing he or she helped someone be more successful.

4. It improves the mentor's self-awareness.

5. It is professionally rejuvenating for the mentor.

6. It allows the mentor to shape his or her legacy.

7. It enhances the mentor's leadership, teaching, coaching, and communication skills.

5.2.4 Building One's Mentoring Skills

Mentoring traditionally means having experienced senior people advising, counseling, and guiding employees toward a longer-term career development. An employee who agonises over which career to pursue or how to navigate office politics might need mentoring.

Mentoring may be formal or informal. Informally, mid- and senior-level mangers may voluntarily help less-experienced employees, for instance, by giving them career advice and helping them to navigate office politics. Many employers also have formal mentoring programs. For instance, the employer may pair protégés with potential mentors and provide training to help mentor and protégés understand their respective responsibilities. Studies show that having a mentor give career-related guidance and act as a sounding board can significantly enhance one's career satisfaction and success.

Mentoring Caveats: For the supervisor, mentoring is both valuable and dangerous. It can be valuable insofar as it allows one to impact, in a positive way, the careers and lives of one's less-experienced subordinates and colleagues. The danger lies on the other side of that same coin. Coaching focuses on daily tasks that you can easily re-learn, so coaching's downside is usually limited. Mentoring focuses on relatively hard-to-reverse longer-term issues, and often touches on the person's psychology like motives, needs, aptitudes, and how one gets along with others. Because the supervisor is usually not a psychologist or a trained career advisor, he or she must be extra cautious in the mentoring advice he or she imparts.

The Effective Mentor: Research on what supervisors can do to be better mentors reveals few surprises. Effective mentors set high standards, are willing to invest the time and effort the mentoring relationship requires, and actively steer protégés into important projects, teams, and jobs. Effective mentoring requires trust, and the level of trust reflects the mentor's professional competence, consistency, ability to communicate and readiness to share control.

On the other hand, the findings on what employers can do to make mentoring programs more effective are somewhat counter intuitive. The findings are summarised as follows.

- **Is mentoring required?** It makes little difference in the extent or quality of mentoring whether the protégés volunteered to take part, or were assigned formally to mentors.
- **Is mentor training to be provided?** Keep it to a minimum. The more hours spent on mentor training, the more mentors reported poorer mentoring relationships. This might be related to resentment about time spent on training or unduly raised expectations.
- **Does distance matter?** No. Participants say men have worked harder at their relationships in order to compensate for the distance.
- **Same or different departments?** Mentoring was more useful when mentors and protégés were in the same department.
- **Big or small difference in rank?** Protégés prefer mentors closer to their own level. This should make first-line supervisors particularly valuable as mentors.

The Protégé's Responsibilities: Effective mentoring is a two-way street. It is important to have effective mentors. However, as the one with the most to gain, the protégé is still largely responsible for making the relationship work. Suggestions for protégés include:

- **Choose an appropriate potential mentor.** The mentor should be objective enough to offer good career advice. Many people seek out someone who is one or two levels above their current boss.

- **Do not be surprised if you are turned down.** Not everyone is willing to undertake this time-consuming commitment.

- **Make it easier for a potential mentor to agree to your request.** Do so by making it clear ahead of time what to expect in terms of time and advice.

- **Respect the mentor's time:** Be selective about the work-related issues that you bring to the table. The mentoring relationship generally should not involve personal problems or issues.

5.2.5 Commitment-oriented Career Development Efforts

The globalisation of the world economy was a boon in many ways. For products and services ranging from cars to computers to air travel, it brought about lower prices, better quality and higher productivity and (in many countries) higher living standards. However, the same cost-efficiencies, belt-tightening, and productivity improvements that globalisation produced also triggered numerous workforce dislocations. The desire for efficiencies drove firms to "do more with less", and with every bankruptcy, buyout and merger, more employees found themselves out of work.

This understandably undermines employer commitment. As noted earlier in this chapter, the "psychological contract" changed. Now, many employees ask, "Why should I be loyal to you if you are just going to dump me when you decide to cut costs again?" To paraphrase the author of the book 'Pack Your Own Parachute', employees today thus tend to think of themselves as free agents, there to do a good job but also to prepare for the next likely move, to another firm. In this environment, many employees expect their employers to provide an opportunity for them to broaden their career options. That is why, as discussed earlier in this chapter, the most attractive proposition an employer can make today is that in five years the employee will have more knowledge and be more employable than now.

It is obvious there are many things that the employer can do to improve the employee's development and career prospects, from job postings and tuition reimbursement to career planning workshops. The main thing is that the employer's career development efforts, taken as a whole, should send the signal that the employer cares about the employee's career success and thus deserves the employee's commitment. Of all the opportunities an employer and supervisor have for supporting employees' career development needs, probably none is as important as a career-oriented appraisal.

Career-oriented Appraisals: In brief, if one uses the performance review only to tell the employee how he or she is doing, one will miss an opportunity to support the employee's career development. Performance appraisals are not just about telling someone how he or she has done. They also provide an opportunity to discuss and link the employee's performance, career interests, and developmental needs into a coherent career plan.

Many employers have formal programs to do this. For example, JCPenney's managerial performance appraisal form contains a listing of all the Penney jobs by title, function, and level that employees could conceivably want to consider. The company trains its supervisors to link the employee's performance, career interests, and corporate needs, and develop a career plan including development activities for the employee.

In Larsen & Toubro, the merit-based performance appraisal system is a critical element of career management. The engineering company, with a unique share holding pattern (no single family or group owns majority shares), explicitly provides opportunity for any engineer who joins as a graduate trainee to eventually become director of the company, provided the person performs consistently. As of March 2010, the majority of executive directors on the board of L&T had joined the company as graduate engineers.

The main thing is to help the manager and employee translate the latter's performance-based experiences for the year into tangible development plans and goals.

While all employees have much in common, a diverse workforce often brings to the workplace some special career development needs. The accompanying "Managing the New Workforce" feature addresses this.

5.3 Managing the New Workforce: Different Career Development Needs

Women and men face different challenges as they advance through their careers. Women report greater barriers (such as being excluded from informal networks), than do men, and greater difficulty getting developmental assignments and geographic mobility opportunities. Women have to be more proactive to get such assignments.

Unfortunately, many career development programs are not consistent with the needs of minority and non-minority women. For example, many such programs underestimate the role played by family responsibilities in many women and men's lives. Similarly, some programs assume that career paths are continuous; however, the need to stop working for a time to attend to family needs often punctuates the career paths of many people. Several types of career development programs, fast-track programs, individual career counselling and career planning workshops are less available to women than to men. Many refer to this totality of subtle and not-so-subtle barriers to women's career progress as the 'glass ceiling'.

Given all this, the most important thing the employer and manager can do is to take the career needs of women and minority employees seriously. Some specific steps include the following.

1. **Eliminate Institutional Barriers:** Many practices, such as required late-night meetings, may seem gender neutral but in fact disproportionately affect women and minorities.

2. **Improve Networking and Mentoring:** To improve female employee's networking opportunities, Marriott International instituted a series of leadership conferences for women. Speakers offered practical tips for career advancement, and shared their experiences. More important, the conferences provided informal opportunities over lunch, for instance, for the Marriott women to meet and forge business relationships. Abolish the 'glass ceiling'. Eliminating 'glass ceiling' barriers requires more than an order from the CEO, because the problem is usually systemic. As one expert puts it, "the roots of gender discrimination are built into a platform of work practices, cultural norms, and images that appear unbiased. People do not even notice them, let alone question them." These range from the late-night meetings mentioned earlier to golf course memberships.

3. **Adopt Flexible Career Tracts:** Inflexible promotional ladders (such as "you must work 8 years of 70-hour weeks to apply for partnership position) can put women, who often have more responsibility for child-raising chores, at a disadvantage. In many large accounting firms, for instance, "more men successfully logged the dozen or so years normally needed" to apply for a position as partner. But fewer women stuck around, so fewer applied for or earned these prized positions." One solution is to institute career tracks (including reduced hours and more flexible year-round work schedules) that enable women to periodically reduce their time at work, but remain on a partner track.

Points to Remember

- **Career management** is a process for enabling employees to better understand and develop their career skills and interests and to use these skills and interests most effectively, both within the company and after they leave the firm.
- Research has shown that certain attitudes are formed early in life to guide many people throughout their careers. These attitudinal syndromes serve to 'anchor' an individual to one or a few related types of career.
- **Five identified career anchors are:**
  1. Managerial Competence
  2. Technical-functional Competence
  3. Security
  4. Creativity
  5. Autonomy-independence

- **A career involves various stages.** The stages are as follows.
  1. Exploratory Stage
  2. Establishment Stage
  3. Maintenance Stage
  4. Decline
- **A well-designed career development programme has the following three stages.**
  1. Career Need Assessment
  2. Career Opportunities
  3. Need-opportunity Alignment
- **Different Methods used by the Employer to enhance Employee Career**
  1. Training
  2. Self-directed Learning
  3. Coaching and Mentoring
  4. Employee Promotion
  5. Job enrichment
  6. Job Rotation and Cross Training
  7. Lateral Moves
  8. Job Aids
- **Mentoring** is a formal or informal relationship established between an experienced, knowledgeable employee and an inexperienced or new employee. The purpose of the mentoring relationship is to help the new employee quickly absorb the organisation's cultural and social norms.

Questions for Discussion

1. Describe the meaning of career management and the role of the organisation in career management.
2. What are the various methods used by the employer to enhance employee career?
3. Explain special issues in career development.
4. Elaborate the benefits of mentoring for employee development.
5. Highlight various innovative employer career initiatives.

Project Questions

1. Although you are responsible for your career, what obligation does the organisation have the plateaued employee whose skills have become obsolescent?
2. Which two of the methods suggested for career enhancement are the most valuable to you? Why?

■■■

Case Studies

Case Study 1

Rameshwar is a manager operation in a mortgage firm based in Kolkata. He reports to the regional manager of the firm based in Bhubaneshwar, Rameshwar narrates his detailed activities.

Rameshwar's job is demanding and he is under tremendous pressure for time. He is a busy executive. He prefers to be precise in his work which is needed more when the pressure of work rises. He has to be systematic and be pin-pointed when he gives instructions to others lest the chances of misinterpretation is ruled out. The cost of misinterpretation is too high for the firm, so Rameshwar can ill-afford any wrong interpretation of information by others (skill in communication and attention to minute details needed).

Rameshwar is a seasoned executive and knows the value of speaking a few words. He is very particular in his choice of words. He thinks before he speaks specially when he apprehends that the things are getting out of hand or messy and chance of misinterpretation is potential (capability to deal with stress). Since the job situation is subject fast changes, he has to remain on his guard to meet the changing exigencies of demanding situation (skill to adapt).

He is required to deal with different persons having different personality types and so these people respond to stresses differently in different situations. So, Rameshwar understands the entire work environment. He, therefore, has to read each person he deals with and keeps his patience and help deal with the working ground of people in his department (aptitude for team working and skill to handle stress and strains).

Staff observes their superior's work behaviour and Rameshwar is a role model for the total group of staff. Staff are trained to be focused on the job, work related conflicts are not seen in the department.

Question:

Analyse the managerial approach of Rameshwar.

Case Study 2

Ghanshayam is an industrial relations manager in ABC manufacturing company located in Delhi NCR. The company employs 4500 artisans, 500 stab's and 1000 executives.

The company has poor worker-management relation ever since the onset of the economic depression in 2007. Although, the company has not suffered losses due to the economic downturn because its products are well-known and established for good quality. Its customer preferences exists for its wide ranging goods and services in white good service in the country. But, its export order from west European market has suffered loss during 2009. As a result, the company had to tap alternate market in south-cost Asian countries which is highly competitive market. In sequence, the company had to face a lot of competition,

In December 2009, the company announced a cut of 0.5 percent, in the work force to the extent of 0.25 percent. This proposal of the company faced stiff agitation from the workers as well as recognised trade unions,

Ghanshayam is an experienced Industrial Relations (IR) manager with high academic achievement from a top ranking Indian management institute. He knows the trick, of the trade related to IR in dealing with the trade unions. He knows that in the existing environment of IR, he must change his style or managing (skill to adjust to changing times/situations). He speaks with confidence in his interaction with trade unions/workers representatives. He is precise and to the point in his work. He has been busy all these days dealing with the unions. He cannot make false promises to the workers on the issue of 0.25% reduction the work force in the next six months which the workers have demanded from the management. A false promise will cost his job and the agitational approach of the union may get translated into works stoppages/stokes. So, he is in dilemma as to what should be his next step (need for negotiating skill, skill in communication and decision-making in adverse condition, managing stress).

In his meetings with the union to win over them with management briefs to implement the drastic step to reduce manpower is a great challenge (skill to win over agitating workers, ability to size tip the situation and understanding the workers mind), So, be discusses the workers demand to stop the cut in manpower with the company's CEO. He knows that if he takes the lead to suggest to the management to extend the management decision to reduce the manpower by 0.2 percent over a period of two years by stopping fresh recruitment for the next 3-4 years for filling up the vacancies created due to natural wastages will satisfy both sides of the management and the workers (presentation skill). In this way, Ghanshayam will succeed to win over the agitating workers and objective of the management also will remain fulfilled (ability to convince the top management/CEO and deal with stressful situations). Ghanshayam succeeded in his design and the problem was solved amicably.

Question

On the basis of above case list out the various competencies required an Industrial relation manager.

Case Study 3
A Mortgage Ranting Company

A mortgage company in the USA launched a paperless mortgage which did not require any documentation from the applicants. The scheme faced stiff competition from the companies arch rivals. In order to beat the competition the company focused on development of its sales forces. The organisation planned to progressively raise: number of its sales associates to operate in the field. But, achieving this plan was an uphill task because of the stiff competition and the nature of the companies unique products and services which needed talented people. There was also a problem of turnover amongst the staff. So the company had to address the high turnover problem among the office staff, There was also an incidence of wide differences in the achievements in sales targets among the offices of the company. On close examination of the problem, the company concluded that its regional managers did not exactly understand what was required to do to get over the downward sales operation,

The company hiring, system did not focus on the specific requirements needed on the job. Hence, the only way out for the company was to develop competency model for sales which could specify the traits needed to be successful on job. The sales competency model is given as follows (Lucia and Lepsinger, 1999):

Criterion for competency model

(i) **Capabilities**

    (a) **Mentally agile:** Capability to address multi-dimensional issues/details, mental agility capability to learn.

    (b) **Reasoning and qualitative ness:** Ability to understand with logic, critically analyze database to conclude, and be at case with qualitative numbers.

    (c) **Thinking out of the box:** Ability to divergent logical thinking to formulate and give unique solution.

(ii) **Personality:**

    (a) **Huge emotional energy:** Be able to keep concentrated and be effective in all favourable and unfavourable conditions.

    (b) **Be tactful/assertive:** Be capable to keep up the motivation and be able to work for long period of time without needing support/superiors.

(iii) **Social skills:**

    (a) **Be capable** to interact with all, displaying respect and warmth to all. Should be able to get on well with all.

    (b) **Self confidence:** Be self-motivated to work for long without supervision.

    (c) **Winner:** Be self-motivated and focused on winning, exceed the set objectives and not lose the winning spirit when counteracting road blocks,

    (d) **Be assertive:** Be able to take on business conditions and show tactfulness diplomatically.

    (e) **High spirited:** Be high spirited, keep up speed and level of performance.

(iv) Sales skills

(a) **Skill of presentation:** Be able to articulate in presentation of ideas/data with groups of all kinds, use audio visual aides in presentations. Be able to perceive the indications coming from the groups. Be smut and keep up perseverance and command the audience.

(b) **Skill for training and development:** Be conversant with training needs/appraisal methods to assess training and development needs. Give training for fulfilling gaps in knowledge and skill, and ensure absorption and implementing new knowledge and motivate learners to learn.

(c) **Skill in selling:** Be capable to build rapport, understand needs and wants of customers, have the skill to sell products, expert/knowledge of features of the product and know performance of the product in terns of customer needs and will orders.

(d) **Skill in solving problem:** Be capable to understand distinction and causes and symptoms. Invite suggestions and ideas and implement them as well as wherever necessary the proposal may be modified. involve the people in problem-solving.

(v) Be knowledgeable:

(a) **Computer knowledge:** Be skilled in computer application in the field of marketing, processing economic information/data, list of prospective clients and client control, etc.

(b) **Knowledge of product:** Be fully knowledgable/expert on companies product and services and related business subjects.

(c) **Financial ability:** Be capable to understand financial aspects. its impact on customer's choice for products, and on the client's client as well as the organisation.

(d) **Competitiveness:** Be knowledgeable about the competing forces/competitors, company's strategies to deal with customers and the products.

The mortgage banking company used the model in the following ways:

(i) The model was adapted in the selection process of the company. Everyone involved in the selection process of sales associate had to work on the same dimension pertaining to high performance on job.

(ii) The competency model was integrated in the system of performance management. This ensured that the sales staff will get coaching and training where needed, besides getting feedback on their sales performance is as well as the skills and knowledge, which are closely related to success on the task. In effect, the newly recruited sales associates where able to achieve high productivity target and their turnover also went down.

Question

Analyse the competency model adopted by the company in detail.

Case Study 4

The Career Planning Programme of Carter Cleaning Company

Career planning has always been a pretty low priority item for Carter Cleaning since "just getting workers to come to work and then keeping them honest is enough of a problem", as Jack likes to say. Yet Jennifer thought, to chart a career planning programme might involve for Carter. A lot of their employees had been with them for years in dead-end jobs and she frankly felt a little bad for them: "perhaps we could help them gain a better perspective on what they want to do", she thought. And she definitely believed that the store management group needed better career direction if Carter Cleaning was to develop and grow.

Questions

1. What mould be the advantages to Carter Cleaning of setting up such a career planning programme?
2. Who should participate in the programme? All employees? Selected employees?
3. Describe the programme you would propose for injecting a career planning and development perspective into the Carter Cleaning Centre.

Case Study 5

Asian Insurance Company Ltd. is one of the largest insurance companies in India with significant market share. The company has been following hierarchical career planning. Employee development is a separate initiative and not linked to career movement of employees. Recently, the company has taken over Jumbo Insurance Ltd. and merged with its operations. Many human resources related issues have cropped up during and after the said merger. This has mainly arisen due to lack of parity in career policies and practices between Asian Insurance Company and Jumbo Insurance Ltd. Jumbo Insurance also has a hierarchical promotion system, but promotions are comparatively slow. This one issue has become a big hurdle in creating a unified work force.

Top management of the insurance company has also realized that unless this issue is amicably resolved, it is difficult to attain, real performance from employees. George Thomson, chief executive of Asian Insurance Company held a meeting of board of directors to discuss this career management problem. One of them suggested to extend Asian's career policy to erstwhile Jumbo employees also and another director disagreed saying the original Asian's employees are not ready to accept this equal treatment. On a detailed discussion, the board finally agreed to use this opportunity to revamp the career policies and create a contemporary, competency centric and organizationally dovetailed career planning and development programme.

Question

Discuss how a career policy and practice can be built, which is most appropriate to Asian Insurance Company in the light of the above described background.

Case Study 6

Sue Ann Scott was a receptionist at the headquarters of a large corporation. A high school graduate, she had no particular skills other than an ability to organise her job duties and a pleasant personality. Unfortunately, she did not have any particular plan for career development; nevertheless, she wanted very much to improve her economic position. Recognising her educational limitations, she began taking accounting courses on a random basis in an evening adult education program.

Scott also took advantage of the corporation's job bidding system by applying for openings that were posted, even though in many instances she did not meet the specifications listed for them. After being rejected several times, she became discouraged. Her depressed spirits were observed by Elizabeth Burroughs, one of the department managers in the corporation. Burroughs invited Scott to come to her office for a talk about the problems she was having. Scott took full advantage of this opportunity to express her frustrations and disappointments. As she unburdened herself, it became apparent both to her and to Burroughs that during interviews she repeatedly apologized for having "only a high school education," an attitude that had probably made it difficult for the interviewers to select her over other candidates who were more positive about their backgrounds and skills. Burroughs suggested that Scott might try taking a more positive approach during her interviews. For example, she could stress her self-improvement efforts at night school and the fact that she was a dependable and cooperative person who was willing to work hard to succeed in the job for which she was applying.

Following Burroughs's advice, Scott applied for a position as invoice clerk, a job for which she felt she was qualified. She made a very forceful and positive presentation during her interview, stressing the favorable qualities she possessed. As a result of this approach, she got the job. While the pay for an invoice clerk was not much more than that for a receptionist, the position did offer an avenue for possible advancement into the accounting field, in which the accounting courses she was taking would be of value.

Questions

1. What are some of the possible reasons Scott did not seek or receive advice from her immediate supervisor?

2. After reviewing the chapter, suggest all possible ways that Scott can prepare herself for career advancement.

Case Study 7

ABC Bank is one of the India's major clearing banks. Over the last decade, the bank has faced an environment that is increasingly competitive and fast moving. The bank has been undergoing a major strategic review of its structure and activities. A key belief has been that greater responsibility for the development and delivery of activities should be passed to front-line employees. Successive voluntary redundancy programmes had made for a relatively young workforce.

Hitherto, career development had equated to promotion through a 17-grade structure. Hence, prior to the redundancies, such promotion could be expected through the grades every 2 to 3 years. Fairly simple manpower planning techniques now reveal a slowing-down in the number of future promotions. A formal integrated career management framework does not currently exist.

Recently, a series of one-day workshops concerning career management at the bank was held by the HR manager for a random selection of managers and employees. One of the key issues highlighted was that career progression was seen as a 'gradist' concept due to the number of grades. This was seen to reduce emphasis on career management issues – such as developmental job moves, sideways job moves, rewards for on-the-job and self-directed development – promoting an entrepreneurial job culture based on knowledge, experience, skill and opportunity and the evolution of a flatter, more flexible organisation structure. It soon became clear that there was little congruence between the fast-moving environment which the bank now faced and career management. Perhaps most important of all, line managers often did not promote development, seeing it as the role of the HR function to develop people and manage careers.

In a follow-up survey of all staff, some of the key findings were as follows:

1. When looking at career issues in the organisation, it is suggested that line managers are not willing to develop staff, particularly 'on the job'
2. The organisation does not readily promote development or on-the-job development
3. The organisation does not help people manage their own careers
4. The organisation does not often explain the career options open to people
5. The organisation needs to devote more resources to helping people to manage their development and career planning.

There is an overall belief that it is important to work for an organisation that allows people to build their own careers, since this:

1. Encourages personal development
2. Allows people to develop by experiencing different fields of work
3. Allows people to develop their existing competencies and skills
4. Provides information on career development
5. Regards career development as important.

Further research about the criteria used for promotions revealed that while individuals wanted promotion decisions to take into account their career development, they believed that they were promoted on the simple basis of suitable vacancies being available.

Furthermore, with regard to whom the system promoted, women felt that expediency was favoured over and above career development.

Questions

1. What are the key issues in the management of careers in this organisation?

2. What suggestions would you make for improving career management in this organization? What are the key roles and responsibilities?

3. How could a competency framework help this organisation plan and manage careers?

■■■

April 2015

Time : 2½ Hours   Maximum Marks : 50

N.B. : (i) All questions carry equal marks.
           (ii) Answer all the questions.

1. "Though the concept of competency got popularity still there are lots of confusion regarding its meaning and application". Explain in detail.

OR

Write in detail KSA Vs. Competency.

2. Explain the various components of Competency.

OR

"HR Generic competency model is the tool for the effective evaluation of employee performance". Explain.

3. What are the different categories in competencies? Describe in detail with examples.

OR

"It is essential to follow the specific steps for developing an effective competency models". Explain.

4. "Career development is an important function". Explain with suitable example.

OR

Describe the different methods of career development.

5. "Employer can lead their organisation towards success by designing an effective career development plan their employees". Discuss.

OR

"Mentoring for Employee Development". Discuss.

■■■